The First Guidebook for Feng Shui Enthusiasts

A Foreword by world-renowned
Feng Shui & Destiny expert
Grand Master Raymond Lo.

Jen Nicomedes

Cover design by CreateSpace, an Amazon.com company
Editing by Valerie Dowdle
Graphics by Clint Moore
Image licenses by iStockPhoto

The author can be reached at:
6207 N Cattletrack Road, Suite 7
Scottsdale, AZ 85250
United States of America
Email: jen@nicomedesrealestate.com
Website: www.fengshuibyjen.com

My first book is dedicated to my mom and dad.

Contents

Foreword

....

by Grand Master Raymond Lo

My students often ask me what qualities one should possess to become a Feng Shui Master. My answer to that is always the same: To study Feng Shui well, one should be passionate about the subject matter, have a strong sense of curiosity and desire to pursue knowledge and truth, have a logical mind for analytical thinking, keep a skeptical attitude to differentiate true knowledge from superstition, and be ethical and responsible.

I first met Jen in July 2013, when she came all the way to Hong Kong from the USA to attend my Four Pillars and I Ching class. I was deeply impressed by her pleasant and humble personality, strong intelligence, and passion to study. I soon discovered not only is she fully equipped with all of the above requirements for an excellent Feng Shui master, but she is also a very responsible and sincere person with an exceptional good memory. While studying closely with me, Jen is devoted to developing her professional Feng Shui and Four Pillars of Destiny consulting business in Arizona, USA. She held a series of successful workshops and established her reputation as a good professional Feng Shui consultant with very positive client feedback. Because she is one of my best and outstanding disciples, I invited and promoted her to become my representative and organizer for my school's professional training program in the USA.

Jen was born and educated in Hong Kong during her childhood, and this gave her a foundation in the Chinese language and culture. This is an obvious advantage, as she can write very good Chinese characters and the Eastern style of thinking still runs in her blood. Jen is also a highly educated girl with good achievements in academic and professional pursuits as a Certified Public Accountant and Compliance Auditor, as well as a licensed property agent. Furthermore, she is also a very good writer. Her articles regularly appear in popular online magazines and websites. She covers a big range of subjects, from Feng Shui, insightful analysis of current social and political issues, to spiritual development of the heart and soul.

Today I am very glad to endorse her first book on Feng Shui. It is a very comprehensive introduction to the subject for people who are enthusiastic in understanding and learning more about this profound ancient Chinese knowledge. I find her style of writing to be very clear, logical, charming, and refreshing. Her approach to this knowledge is very natural and easy, like breathing in fresh air. I believe Jen's great talent in writing helps a lot in explaining this complicated knowledge of Feng Shui, and her pleasant and sincere style makes this book comfortable to read and easy to follow.

I am so excited to recommend this very useful and friendly book to anyone who is interested in learning more about the popular subject of Feng Shui. This book interests me in particular as Jen comes from a highly educated Western background, and her writing very much reflects her insight into all aspects of Feng Shui, especially from an objective and logical view point.

The book covers the classical traditional Chinese Feng Shui knowledge, as well as the Western views and ideas about the subject. It offers a very clear insight of the structure and essence of Classical Feng Shui (as practiced among Chinese Feng Shui masters), along with a wider scope showing a clear picture of its subsequent evolution, development, and variations as it is adopted in the Western world.

I heartily congratulate Jen for her success in producing such a good book and I very much look forward to her great contribution to the Feng Shui industry.

Grand Master Raymond Lo
Hong Kong
January 2014

Acknowledgements

"Gratitude is the memory of the heart." – JEAN BAPTISTE MASSIEU

My heart space is joyfully occupied by a band of "Earth Angels" who have helped make this book a dream come true.

Valerie Dowdle, my trusted editor. Thank you for being instrumental during my years of writing. I appreciate our commonality in holding the "art of words" to the highest regard. I admire your sharp eyes and fearless conviction. Thank you for always pushing me to produce only the best writing.

Karen Moore, my soul sister, who gifted me the Feng Shui book that would forever change my life. You are the backbone behind so much of my growth – personally and creatively. Thank you for infusing my life with inspiration and humanity.

To Michael Coakes for my beautiful logo design and to Clint Moore, the gifted artist behind my website design and the graphics in my book. Thank you both for sharing so much of your creative spirit with me.

To my Arizona support team, the journey truly began here. Thank you to Lori Newcomb, Kim Olson, Carrie Rittling, Cat Stevenson, Summer Warner, and especially to Mike Dufour for his confidence, unwavering trust, and unconditional support for making me believe in the strength of my dreams. My Gopi Sisters on the Ranch: Tristan Gandolfi, Rebecca Lammersen, Logan Milliken, Lindsey Smith, Mary Thomas, and Dusti Van Tilborg.

A very special shout-out to "Angel" Angie Krause for helping me *see* a whole new light about myself and the world around me. Your gift to me was – and is – the doorway to all of my receiving.

I am also deeply grateful to all of my clients and to those who have attended my workshops and training seminars. Your curiosity, enthusiasm, and open-mindedness for this art inspire me every day to dig deeper and be the best practitioner I can be. It is because of you that I am able to share this ancient art responsibly and with integrity – with this book and in my practice and teaching. I am humbled by your trust and touched by your personal stories, and especially honored to be welcomed inside your beautiful, sacred homes.

Lastly, to my teacher and mentor, Grand Master Raymond Lo, words cannot express my deep gratitude for your generosity, kindness, wisdom, trust, and heartfelt support. I appreciate the boundless gift of your time in teaching me every day, diligently reviewing and ensuring my book upholds the integrity of the Eastern tradition that you and I both hold so dear. Above all, I cherish our lifelong friendship and learning adventures together.

Preface

My Feng Shui Calling

> *"Twenty years from now you will be more disappointed by the things you didn't do than by the ones you did do. So throw off the bowlines. Sail away from the safe harbor. Catch the trade winds in your sail. Explore. Dream. Discover."* — MARK TWAIN

As a little girl growing up in Hong Kong, I was surrounded by the culture and people that embody the spirit of Feng Shui.

I was kind of an odd kid. My deeply curious mind led me to ask disparate questions you wouldn't expect from the mouth of a seven-year-old. Philosophy, science, and metaphysics… I wanted the "why" and the "what else" of everything I saw around me.

When I was 13, my family and I left my native Hong Kong for the U.S., leaving behind the history and culture of my upbringing to start my new Western life.

Over the next 20-odd years, this departure from my true self – and origin – eventually took its toll.

By 27, I was in a rut. I had a successful corporate career – on paper – but felt trapped in a job that lacked passion and meaning. That's what happens when you spend 90 hours a week crunching numbers alone in a windowless room! I was desperately looking for ways to expand intellectually while also serving others purposefully. I looked for signs, tried different things, and kept an open mind.

One day, out of the blue, a dear friend gifted me a Feng Shui book. That gift literally changed the course of my life – not just over the next few years, but forever.

I left my corporate life (and paycheck) behind to seek a new life as an entrepreneur. People say it was brave. But it was the scariest thing I've ever done.

And the best.

Someone once told me my decision to work in Chinese Metaphysics is an "ironic twist of fate." But in fact, embracing my life's work in Feng Shui felt a lot like coming home – becoming the person I was always meant to be.

THE BOOK AND HOW IT ALL BEGAN

After I completed my initial Feng Shui training, I wanted to know more (and more). But it seemed the deeper I looked for answers, the more confused I became.

There's a lot of people in the Feng Shui community who take it all on faith. I was never any good at that. If I can't explain something analytically, it's not much use to me.

Intuitively I understood what it all meant. But how could it be explained?

There's a tremendous lack of scientific analysis in Feng Shui literature. The answers are there, but you have to do your own digging – a lot of it. So I became relentless.

I needed the *science* behind the philosophy… the intricate techniques behind the methods… the history and origins of the authentic practice… and above all, the bigger picture – much bigger than simply looking at the four walls of a property or moving a few pieces of furniture around.

One of the more pressing questions I had was how this complex and sophisticated system could be watered down to provide simple, quick fixes. If Qi is the driving force behind the goal of Feng Shui, then what is it and where did it come from? Could "bad" energy be addressed without considering the human aspects living in the home? And what was it about that famous "red door?"

In my search for these answers lies the genesis of the book you're about to read.

DOES FENG SHUI STILL MATTER?

My next question was: Does this ancient practice still matter in the 21st century?

(I ask this question here because you may have it too.)

The answer is YES.

Regardless of our cultural, religious, geographical, and personal differences, every human being on the planet today shares the same basic needs. And they're the same ones our ancestors had some 6,000 years ago (when Feng Shui started to take shape: Food, water, shelter, security… and *happiness*).

We all seek happiness, one way or another. And we all want to enjoy the safety and comforts of our homes. The only obvious difference is we now live in a more technologically advanced and materialistic society. We all have more of everything. But our needs are the same.

Irrespective of the change in age, Feng Shui is still very much an important and relevant practice, not only to help us achieve comfort and harmony, but to also understand our environment and ourselves.

It may sound mystical, but there are no magic tricks to applying Feng Shui. It is solely based on the energy flow of the space, the time, and the residences occupying the space, as well as the energy in the environment. Feng Shui lets you manipulate this flow to pursue your goals, whether it is in constructing a new property, rearranging the items in your room, or seeking to increase your personal happiness within a space where you spend a lot of time.

I've seen it work "magic" for clients and for myself.

AN EDUCATION THAT NEVER ENDS

Happily, I got my answers.

Upon completing my initial studies at the Western School of Feng Shui and Mastery Academy of Chinese Metaphysics, I went on to continue the most pivotal part of my training in Classical Feng Shui, BaZi (Four Pillars of Destiny), and I Ching Divination with Grand Master Raymond Lo at Raymond Lo School of Feng Shui and Destiny in Hong Kong – back in my native homeland. The exposure and knowledge I gained from these experiences filled in a lot of the missing holes for me, both as a Feng Shui enthusiast and a professional. My ongoing studies in Chinese Metaphysics took me around the world, to places like Singapore, Dubai, Tokyo, and Australia.

Most notably, my relationship with Grand Master Lo – both as his apprentice and friend – was instrumental in the way I choose to practice Classical Feng Shui. What's more, it gave me deep insight into the importance of keeping up with learning, staying curious, and safeguarding the integrity of the practice.

In 2011, I launched my own Feng Shui consulting practice. It's my personal mission to preserve the authenticity of the Eastern art, here, in our Western world. That's what this book is all about.

This book is not intended to hone you into a Feng Shui practitioner in a few hours of reading. That's just not possible. Many professional Feng Shui practitioners, including myself, dedicate hundreds of hours each year to learn it properly, doing so under the careful guidance of a master.

Feng Shui is an ongoing education. It has a beginning but no ending.

But it is my hope that this book will be your beginning – a kind of layman's introduction to Feng Shui. In that spirit, I keep things simple, easy to follow, with practical examples… and always include the science that makes Feng Shui real.

In the next chapters, I'll help you learn the difference between Classical and Contemporary Feng Shui, demystify and debunk the myths and misconceptions, and demonstrate to you how you can benefit from incorporating Feng Shui in your life.

You will see from the chapter outline that the bulk of the topics are on Classical Feng Shui. This is the traditional, original practice. However, I have also included discussions covering several popular topics on Contemporary Feng Shui, including Space Clearing and the 8 Aspirations Map.

My aim here is to simplify the concepts behind the practice and to also provide a landscape that is easy for anyone – beginners and enthusiasts – to understand and embrace... so we can all get a little closer to happiness.

Enjoy!
Jen Nicomedes
Scottsdale, Ariz.
January 2014
www.FengShuibyJen.com

chapter 1

· ·

WHEN TO APPLY FENG SHUI

Feng Shui can greatly benefit you throughout your life, but it's particularly powerful to harness it before or during certain "transition" periods:

· ·

WHEN YOU CHANGE YOUR LIVING SPACE

- You are moving into a new place, such as a home, apartment, office, or retail space.
- You are building a new house or condominium.
- You are remodeling your existing home or office space.
- You are purchasing a new place.
- You are preparing to sell your home.
- You are merging homes because you're moving in together with a partner or getting married.

WHEN YOUR RELATIONSHIPS OR HOME LIFE CHANGE

- There has been a death in the family or among your close friends.
- You recently got divorced or had a break-up.
- You need some special self-healing or self-care.
- You want to attract new love or strengthen a current relationship.
- You want to invite new friends, mentors, clients, partners, and teachers into your life.
- You are surrounded by clutter that is weighing you down.
- Your space is chaotic and you need to feel grounded again.
- You are looking for fresh direction on achieving and realizing your goals and dreams.

WHEN YOU NEED A CHANGE IN YOUR CAREER AND/OR FINANCES

- You feel "stuck" in your career.
- You are stressed and want to restore balance.
- You want to increase your cash flow or attract more business opportunities.
- You want a promotion or to take your career or business endeavors to the next level.
- You are in a creative rut.
- You are experiencing a sudden bout of money "going out the door."

WHEN YOUR HEALTH AND FAMILY SITUATION IS IN FLUX

- You want to have a baby.
- You are struggling with new or ongoing health issues.
- You are suffering from depression.

- You often feel tired or experience lack of energy.
- You are unmotivated to care for others or for yourself.

Part of this material was originally written by Jen Nicomedes and published on MindBodyGreen.com on January 10, 2013.

chapter 2

DEBUNKING THE MYTHS, MYSTERIES, AND MISCONCEPTIONS

In the last four decades, Feng Shui has shifted from a quiet, strictly Eastern practice into a cultural activity on the global scene. Although the reason for its emergence is not clear, there's a lot of speculation.

For one, there are more Westerners traveling to Asian countries and bringing back with them the knowledge of Chinese cultures to their homeland. More information on Feng Shui has become more accessible with the Internet, too. There are more Asian immigrants integrating their native traditions in their newly adopted country. It has also been attributed to the aftermath of the Chinese Cultural Revolution.

Whatever the reasons might be, it's now a definite part of the modern cultural zeitgeist for people from Asia to the United States and beyond.

That's wonderful! The more people that know about and practice Feng Shui, the better.

However, there is a downside to the sudden popularity of Feng Shui. The authentic meaning of the practice gets lost and muddled up, due to human misinterpretation, misunderstanding, and misuse.

This is especially true in the West. Because the West lacks proximity to the Asian culture and traditional practice of Chinese Metaphysics, I believe many new and mainstream ideas took root among the facts, adding to the confusion. As I practice this Eastern tradition in the West, I find people are often unclear about what Feng Shui is, including its true function and purpose. Some people think it's all about moving around furniture. Others even think it's bogus – some kind of a New Age scam.

I'm going to clear that all up for you.

This section of the book is dedicated to introducing to you the basic fundamentals and definition of Feng Shui. At the same time, we will debunk the myths, mysteries, and misconceptions around Feng Shui. What it is and what it is not. This is an important first step, because in order to learn Feng Shui properly, you must appreciate its rich history. You'll learn the beginnings and the original intent of the practice. This is not only an essential basis for the proper use and application of Feng Shui, but it also forms the backbone of all learning standards for Chinese Metaphysics as a whole.

So before you begin, I wholeheartedly encourage you to release everything you think you know about Feng Shui... and start over by exploring its fascinating history from the very beginning.

Ready? Let's go.

FIGURE 1: CHINESE CHARACTERS FOR *FENG SHUI*.

DISSECTING AN ANCIENT PRACTICE: A BRIEF HISTORY

Feng Shui (pronounced "*fung schway*") literally translates to mean "Wind-Water."

Feng Shui is a very ancient knowledge. Although some of the details of its origin have been lost to history, ancient classic texts indicate that the practice began with primitive people searching for safe dwellings. This "body of knowledge" was developed based on their observation of their relationship with the land where they lived.

Feng Shui is a complex and sophisticated metaphysical system that was developed around 2700 B.C. when the legendary Yellow Emperor Huang Ti is credited with inventing the Feng Shui Compass (Luo Pan). However, the knowledge of Feng Shui goes as far back as 4500 B.C. The fundamental knowledge and principles for understanding Feng Shui can be traced to this time, which is also the time of ruler Fu Xi (who invented the Eight Trigrams and the Early Heaven Ba Gua).

The study of I Ching Divination emerged during the Warring States Period (475-221 B.C.). That's when Chinese cosmology and philosophy like Confucianism and Taoism, as well as the theories of Yin and Yang and the Five Elements, began to take shape.

Feng Shui truly began to flourish during the Tang Dynasty (618-907 A.D.) when Master Yang Yun Sung (834-900) wrote many books on Feng Shui. (Master Yang is regarded as the Grandfather – or Grand Teacher – of Feng Shui because he is often credited with inventing the Heaven Plate and the 72 Dragon ring on the Luo Pan.) Evidence of Feng Shui work can now be seen in the building of many palaces, villages, and tombs from that time.

Feng Shui continued to see rapid development during the Five Dynasties and 10 Kingdoms era (907-960) despite the demise of the Tang Dynasty.

Although Feng Shui has seen its evolvement over time, the Sung Dynasty (960-1279) catapulted the practice to its maturity. Most of its applications and methods solidified during this time, and Feng Shui masters, teachers, students, and books abounded. This is also the time of the distinct separation of the predominant schools: the San Yuan and San He Schools of Feng Shui (more on this in Chapter 3).

By the Ming Dynasty (1368-1644), every building was being constructed based on the theory and principles of Feng Shui.

The end of the Ming Dynasty and the start of the Qing Dynasty (1644-1911) brought one of mankind's greatest architectural designs that still stands today: The Forbidden City. This masterpiece is located in the center of China's capital in Beijing, and it exemplifies the fundamental ideals of Classical Feng Shui.

NOTE FROM JEN: *If you are interested in exploring the history of Feng Shui in more detail, Master Stephen Skinner's book "History of Feng Shui" is an excellent reference material.*

FENG SHUI FOR THE DEAD

In the old days, Feng Shui was also called *Kan Yu*, meaning "the Observation of Qi between Heaven and Earth," a terminology used to locate the best burial sites for the dead. (This original form of practice is also popularly referred to as Yin Feng Shui or Yin Houses.) The use of the early form of Feng Shui, or geomancy, in picking gravesites and tombstones can also be traced back to an early source of Feng Shui doctrine called *The Book of Burial*, written by Taoist philosopher Guo Pu (276-324 A.D.) of the Jin Dynasty (265-420).

This type of practice is deeply rooted in Chinese tradition. Why?

For one thing, "ancestor luck" is a significant Chinese cultural belief. It continues to play an important role in modern society today. Chinese believe that by burying their loved ones at the right resting spot, not only does it reinforce unity with their ancestors, but it also ensures the family's fortune and prosperity for future generations to come.

Also, the circumstances of burial held great significance in ancient times. This idea is much like pharaohs building massive tombs or pyramids to protect the deceased. In Egyptian history, the process of mummifying and constructing pyramids was thought to protect the pharaoh's body eternally and to avoid cosmic disturbances in the fortune of his son (also his successor).

THE EARLY YEARS OF FENG SHUI

Much of the practice was originally a closely guarded secret. It was not for public knowledge. Feng Shui masters were only permitted to share and practice the art with emperors and other nobles.

Even so, while many books have been written by masters and students during the ancient times, most of the knowledge and techniques were transmitted anecdotally and through practical exercises, and were passed on to only a very selective few – their disciples or descendants.

APPLYING THE PRACTICE TO THE LIVING

It is still unclear whether Yin House Feng Shui preceded Yang House Feng Shui (as there are conflicting conclusions among scholars and historians). However, history has shown that Feng Shui was (and is) a vital component to the dwellings of people.

This important and significant discovery has led to the widespread use of Feng Shui to locate proper building sites – not just for residences, but also to construct palaces, government buildings, and other public monuments.

As you continue to explore the fundamentals, you will appreciate the root of the practice is founded on the basic concept of **Qi**. That's the idea that nature and the land you stand on is alive, and that people are in a constant exchange of energy with each other and with their environment. If you were to build or move into a home, for instance, you are essentially accessing the Qi influences in the environment. Those may have a positive or adverse impact on your health and wealth.

Because the Chinese believed in amassing good luck from the environment, the practice of Feng Shui became the means to harness positive Qi for their homes, and this became an important integration in their culture.

THE CULTURAL REVOLUTION WAS A SETBACK FOR FENG SHUI

The Great Proletarian Cultural Revolution took place in the People's Republic of China in 1966. It stemmed from China's younger generation wanting to purge the nation of what was known as the "Four Olds:"

- Old customs
- Old culture
- Old habits
- Old ideas

Feng Shui, being an ancient practice and an integral part of Chinese culture, was suppressed on account of its more mythical and mysterious elements. As a result, much of the literature and important works and documents on Feng Shui were destroyed during the Revolution.

During this time, many Feng Shui masters fled to nearby Asian countries, such as Taiwan, Hong Kong, and Malaysia. And thank goodness they did! The legacy of the ancient practice only managed to survive this way.

When the Revolution ended around 1976, it was only then the practice of Feng Shui became popular again and was reintroduced in these countries. Although many masters have remained loyal to the authentic principles of Feng Shui, some have gone on to develop an updated version of Feng Shui in order to assimilate with other non-Chinese cultures, to incorporate other personal religious or superstitious beliefs, or to introduce a new "old" idea in their own way.

At this writing, China has slowly allowed the practice of Feng Shui to reemerge after its long ban. However, the practice is not as open or widespread as they are in countries like Hong Kong, Malaysia, and other parts of Southeast Asia.

The origins of Feng Shui are fundamentally shaped from generation to generation through the cultural paradigm. So it's no surprise that it continues to have a close tie with Chinese culture and tradition. However, Classical Feng Shui does not depend on its cultural aspects, geography, or socioeconomic and political structure, religion, or superstitious beliefs. The essence and foundation of Feng Shui can (and should) be synthesized with other bodies of knowledge and philosophies, because it can be applied equally well to meet the specific requirements of societies and cultural ideals anywhere in the world.

Knowledge has no boundaries. And this is the crux of Classical Feng Shui.

NOTE FROM JEN: *Feng Shui teacher Joey Yap once famously quipped, challenging his students and skeptics alike: "You don't have to turn your house or place of business into a Chinese restaurant to practice or reap the benefits of Feng Shui!"*

QI AND GOING BEYOND THE DEFINITION OF A "HOME"

Now we talk about the concept of Qi. And here's where some people get utterly lost or even go off the rails. So I want to let you know right up front: If you want to learn and apply Feng Shui effectively, there are two prerequisites.

First, **you have to understand and believe that nature and land are living bodies that contain an invisible force with the ability to influence and affect life and the environment**. That's Qi.

When the Ancient Chinese understood the basic concept that vital energy is the driving force to good life, it meant using the natural and omnipresent force of the land's Qi to support and nourish the home, mind, body, and spirit. (More on Qi on Chapter 4.)

Second, **you must learn to view a home beyond the basic definition**. For some, a home may simply be a structural building with four or more walls, a solid foundation, and a roof above. A place to cook, sleep, and take shelter from the harsh conditions. For many purposes, that's a fine definition. To practice Feng Shui, though, you have to cultivate your thinking about what a home really means, regardless of if you own, rent, or share living quarters with other people.

Here's how I think of it…

Do you remember the 1992 film "Far and Away" starring Tom Cruise and Nicole Kidman? The plot followed an Irishman's spirited race to claim a plot of land in the Wild West. In doing so, it meant that he was finally a free man of equal stature in society. It would let him settle down, raise a family, and live.

A Feng Shui home is exactly just that. It goes beyond its basic functionality of a home – to eat, sleep, store your belongings. It symbolizes and translates to wealth and security. For centuries in history, people have waged wars to defend their land and assets, and these homes were also among some of the biggest conquests. A home not only shelters and keeps you safe from the goings-on of your external environment, but it is also a place of sanctuary. It replenishes your personal energy, nurtures your dreams, and welcomes abundance. Your home is ultimately a place of safety, comfort, and power. Doesn't that sound nice?

This is one of the many reasons people incorporate the principles of Feng Shui in their homes.

NOTE FROM JEN: *The practice of Feng Shui begins with creating a healing home – a place where Qi is flowing pleasantly and harmoniously.*

SPIRITUALITY, SUPERSTITION, RELIGION, OR SCIENCE?

Contrary to popular belief, the tradition of Feng Shui has absolutely nothing to do with man-made object placements, charms, trinkets, symbols, crystals, amulets, chanting, praying, or interior decorating.

Some of these misconceptions are derived from modern-day interpretations. Unfortunately, they have turned into a diluted approach to commercialized sales of so-called "Feng Shui gadgets" and quick fixes.

Many people, especially in the West, resonate with having object affirmations in their environment. They need to be able to see and feel something to know it's working. While this element should not be ignored, the most important lesson here is being able to distinguish where the differences lie. After all, scientific studies have proven that certain colors, as well as verbal and object affirmations have positive psychological effects, thereby influencing an individual's perspective of his or her life and environment. However, this idea is incomplete. It only covers one aspect of the practice of Chinese Metaphysics. (We will explore the idea of the Cosmic Trinity in Chapter 5.)

Of course, different Feng Shui schools have different priorities. In Chapter 3, you will begin to understand how some systems place heavy emphasis on science and formulas, while others are formed on the basis of personal spiritual development, intuition, object affirmations, and even religion.

While each factor – spirituality, superstition, religion, and science – has a unique basis for their designation and purpose, it is important to define what they mean first. That's how you will accurately decode the foundation of Feng Shui and learn to recognize their differences.

Spirituality: A spiritual practice involves going "within" and discovering the self that affects the human spirit, as opposed to material or physical objects. Therefore, the experience is not a tangible one. It generally relates to a person's solo transformation or spiritual awakening.

Superstition: Superstition is normally associated with folklore and legends, passed down through generations. It may stem from religious or cultural beliefs. This belief system may also be voodoo, magical, or mythical.

Religion: A religion is a set of systems in which a person believes in and worships of a supernatural or higher power, commonly known as god or other deities and divinities.

Science: The word "science" is derived from the Latin word meaning "knowledge." This is a systematic organization of knowledge that strives to study, rationally explain, and logically apply a particular subject matter.

From the definitions provided above, you can see how the first three – spirituality, superstition, and religion – are unique and specific to each person with prejudice. In other words, they mean different things to different people. As such, the experience and outcome will vary from one to the next.

On the other hand, science is simply a matter of fact. It is a logical and practical approach, and the application is objective. It's the same every time. In Feng Shui, it is understood that no two people are alike; similarly, no two houses are alike. However, the application of the <u>principles</u> of the authentic practice of Feng Shui – which is based on the concept of Qi – is always the same, regardless of time, space, the property, the person, culture, society, status, wealth, goals, and spiritual or religious beliefs.

So if you must define Feng Shui, the shortest answer to that – no matter what system of Feng Shui you apply – it is an ancient Chinese knowledge used to study the Qi (energy) flow of the environment. The methods and application of techniques – whether that is through the use of formulaic models, object placements, science, or spirituality – will depend on the <u>type</u> of Feng Shui system you are using.

NOTE FROM JEN: *The traditional, classical practice of Feng Shui leaves no guesswork. It is a logical, practical, and product-free system. However, if you are indeed a spiritual, religious, or superstitious individual and want to incorporate Feng Shui in your life, it is perfectly fine to combine them! The key lesson here is being able to recognize the differences between the core principles of the classic practice and your personal beliefs.*

TWO THINGS FENG SHUI IS NOT!

First, Feng Shui cannot, must not, and should not be understood as some kind of "magic."

As a Feng Shui consultant, I meet with a lot of people who are on different life paths. Some are transitioning between changes smoothly. Others are coping with difficulties. In both cases, it is my professional responsibility to carefully navigate the implementation of the Feng Shui practice... and that includes making sure they understand it is not a cure-all for life's messy challenges.

Feng Shui can help you take control of your life, achieve balance, make positive changes, and achieve your goals and dreams, but it won't do any of that *for* you. When we explore the concept of the Cosmic Trinity in Chapter 5, you will see that you and your actions play an equal and vital role in influencing your life.

So it is with extreme care that I caution both my readers and clients to purge the impression that Feng Shui will erase all your problems or turn you into a millionaire overnight!

Second, Feng Shui is not a one-time event. It's not a permanent fix that you can apply and then forget about.

Change is the only thing that is constant in life (we'll explore this concept in Chapter 9). Because time passes, the energy cycles also shift. People change too. Your goals and relationships will change, your health and work dynamic will change, and your needs and dreams will also change. This is a normal progression as you experience the ups and downs of your life's path. Moreover, your environment will change. Your job may relocate you to a new town, or you may decide to move elsewhere to raise a family. You may consider moving into a different space or renovating your existing space.

Life is never static, and as such, the application of Feng Shui must be revisited to accurately assess the Qi in your environment and adjust your surroundings to align with your current and future endeavors.

chapter 3

THE THREE SCHOOLS

> *"When you know better, you do better."* — MAYA ANGELOU

Feng Shui is not a singular practice. There are many schools and systems that place an emphasis on different techniques and application. In fact, you may even know Feng Shui as a result of a combination of the schools.

To understand how and where they differ, I want to highlight the three primary systems most commonly practiced today.

Let's jump right in.

SCHOOL #1: CLASSICAL FENG SHUI

As the name implies, Classical Feng Shui is the traditional, Eastern practice.

Perhaps one of the most obvious differences that set Classical Feng Shui apart from the other schools is that it is a macro, or "outward-in," practice that includes the consideration for the environment, time, and direction of the property (or space) in a typical assessment. Under the branch of Classical Feng Shui, there are two predominant sub-systems: Forms Feng Shui and Compass Feng Shui.

Forms School

Forms Feng Shui, or Landscape Feng Shui, is thought to be the oldest Feng Shui system, emphasizing on the natural landforms – or forms – surrounding the property. When I say "landforms," I'm talking about the visual shapes and contours of the environment, including the mountains, terrains, topography, lakes, rivers, and other bodies of water, as well as man-made objects, such as nearby buildings and roads.

Master Yang Yun Sung is credited with expanding the theories of Forms Feng Shui in the 9th century. Although actual documentations of his teachings are scarce, he left a legacy of classical texts on Landscape Feng Shui, including an emphasis on the importance of selecting auspicious sites that have the dragon's energy, or "Dragon's Breath," where vital Qi is located. This revelation subsequently contributed to the importance of the careful examination of the shape of land formations.

NOTE FROM JEN: *Master Yang is also credited for his contribution of many formulas used in Compass School. Because his teachings were so secretive, many Feng Shui masters inherited the knowledge through oral tradition and subsequently interpreted his methods in their own way, eventually leading to the split into the San He and San Yuan Schools.*

With the invention of the magnetic Feng Shui compass, or Luo Pan, many Feng Shui masters became skilled astronomers. They studied the influences of the star constellations as well as the directional flow of energy fields on earth – where energy would gather, collect, and disperse. As such, the goal of a Forms Feng Shui assessment can be summarized as threefold:

1. Observe the natural environment and evaluate the directional divisions of the external features surrounding a property,
2. Understand how the earth's energy is influenced from above (heaven), and
3. Assess the Qi quality in order to identify where the positive or negative Qi-collecting features are in order to access (or avoid) them.

This technique emphasizes achieving harmony between heaven, man, and earth. And it is a fairly straightforward system.

Because Forms Feng Shui is primarily an external assessment, this system is especially useful if you are looking for a plot of land to build a home, office building, school, or landmark (long before you begin to consider the architectural and interior design of the property).

Nowadays, most people do not have the luxury or the financial means to build a home from the ground up – or the ability to move around on a whim. Also, it is quite common for people to purchase or move into previously owned or pre-constructed homes and other rental-type properties. This is especially true in the West.

That's perfectly okay.

As time progresses, people and their homes evolve. So has Feng Shui. A well-trained Feng Shui practitioner makes use of all available resources, tools, and techniques to assess the Qi quality of the environment. There is no such thing as the "perfect house" in a "perfect environment" for all of eternity. We use Forms to assess the Qi quality surrounding a property for its long-term and long-lasting effects to withstand the dynamic changes of time.

More on Forms Feng Shui on Chapter 10.

Compass School

While Forms School focuses on the physical landscape configuration of the environment, Compass School focuses on assessing the abstract energies that cannot be seen with the naked eye.

Compass School is more complex and has many subsets. First of all, Compass School can be divided into two types: Yang House and Yin House. Yang House represents dwellings for people, and Yin House represents burial sites for the dead. The techniques and applications used for each type are also different. Primarily, Flying Star and Eight Mansion Feng Shui are considered the most influential formulaic methods used for Yang House (you'll get an introduction to both of these later in the book). And the two main classical systems for Yin House are San He and San Yuan.

All of these systems emphasize the use of formulaic calculations – rather than the external physical landforms – to determine how Qi affects you and your home. Therefore, it is considered a more dynamic practice. It has quick and short-term effects, prompting the Feng Shui fortune of a house to continuously change as time passes (i.e., the quality of Qi changes with time).

Many of the mathematical models used under Compass School are derived from the ancient classics known as the Yi Jing (or I Ching), and we will explore these concepts throughout the book. And it is important to note that the primary difference between San He and San Yuan is that San He ignores the time factor in the calculation; therefore, the formula mainly focuses on the facing direction of the building.

All formulaic systems are also based on direction, which incorporates the use of a Feng Shui compass known as the Luo Pan (see Chapter 8). In my opinion, a serious Classical Feng Shui practitioner should also examine the astrological charts of the residents occupying the space, making it a more powerful and accurate assessment in determining how certain people will react and respond to the shifts in energy. (This practice is known as BaZi or The Four Pillars of Destiny, and it deserves a whole book unto itself!)

It is important to emphasize that Forms and Compass Schools are not necessarily two separate schools; rather, they should be viewed as two aspects of Feng Shui – one relates to the physical formations of the surrounding, and the other refers to the abstract, invisible influences affected by time and space (directions).

NOTE FROM JEN: *Both Forms and Compass Schools are equally compelling and effective, and you don't need to choose between them. While both schools have their merits and drawbacks, they are not meant to be an either/ or approach. A good Classical Feng Shui practitioner should understand both schools and may choose to place an emphasis on one or the other, and recognize that Forms and Compass go together, but simply differ in priority depending on the needs and situation of the client. You can think of them as hardware and software. They serve different functions and cannot be meaningful unless they work together. Therefore, you will often find serious Classical Feng Shui practitioners understand, practice, and apply **both** theories in a traditional assessment.*

SCHOOL #2: BLACK HAT SECT TANTRIC BUDDHISM FENG SHUI (BTB)

Black Hat, or "BTB," is shorthand for Black Hat Sect Tantric Buddhism Feng Shui.

This style was developed around the '70s by the late Chinese Grand Master Lin Yun Rinpoche. He was considered the one who first introduced and pioneered Feng Shui in the West. Black Hat is also one of the most commonly used systems in the United States.

The school combines the essence and philosophy of Tibetan Buddhism, Taoism, Confucianism, holistic healing, transcendentalism, divination, psychology, and Classical Feng Shui. Clearly, there's a lot going on here.

Many Black Hat Feng Shui practitioners and enthusiasts say the practice is a spiritual and holistic experience, and sometimes even a religious one. It combines the art of meditation by quieting and centering the mind in order to intuitively *feel* the space and its energy. Many practitioners and enthusiasts also perform rituals, chants, mantras, and other affirmations to bless their dwellings or to "call in" the Qi.

While the Black Hat school honors some of the Eastern heritage of the traditional practice, one of the key distinctions is that it does not consider the use of a compass. It does not assess the external environment, the property's location, or house facing directions, as an absolute. Black Hat practice uses the Eight Aspirations Map as its primary tool and is not otherwise a geomantic system. More on the Eight Aspirations Map in Chapter 14.

Since Black Hat is a non-directional practice (wherein the traditional cardinal directions are not observed), the Map is laid out the same way — no matter where the Main Door of the property faces — for all types of properties. Instead of orienting the house with the Feng Shui compass, the Eight Aspirations Map is oriented to the entryway in any room every time. As you can imagine, it relies less on directional energies, landforms, and astrology than Classical Feng Shui. The internal orientation of the door is what matters here.

Black Hat is a popular form, especially in the West. But many traditional Feng Shui practitioners in Asia regard this adaptation as inauthentic, because it grossly deviates from the traditional roots of the classical practice. It often gets ridiculed and challenged for its methods.

One of the main criticisms of Black Hat is that it was invented to make Feng Shui "easy." The lack of consistency and oversimplified application means it is not always as black and white. Primarily, the Feng Shui assessment of a space is subjective to the person performing the evaluation.

Also, many Black Hat practitioners are often deeply spiritual and/or religious individuals, blending or incorporating their personal beliefs into the practice of Feng Shui. This is one of the reasons Feng Shui gets mislabeled as a religion rather than the logical, metaphysical science it is.

NOTE FROM JEN: *Black Hat is considered a micro, non-directional practice that focuses only on orienting the house with the Eight Aspirations Map to the entryway of any door. Qi quality is assessed through a hybrid of religious, philosophical, spiritual, and psychological theories without observing the use of a compass or considering time, direction, or astrological details of the residents.*

SCHOOL #3: NEW AGE FENG SHUI
New Age Feng Shui has many names, including Modern, Western, or Intuitive Feng Shui.

As the name denotes, this system of Feng Shui is "newer." The practice was developed sometime around the early 1990s and is the Western adaption. It borrows and utilizes the Eight Aspirations Map from Black Hat. It also emphasizes products as enhancers – things like crystals, figurines, and talismans, interior designing with colors, shapes, and textures, object placements, and the practice of personal intuition.

This is perhaps the most oversimplified approach to Feng Shui. Many traditional practitioners regard it as "watered down."

Many untrained enthusiasts employ some form of New Age Feng Shui techniques in their homes. Often they may mistake them as the authentic practice of the Eastern tradition. This contributes to the modern-day misconceptions about the practice. Skeptics of Feng Shui often give anecdotes relating the many inconsistencies and conflicting advice they've heard from different New Age Feng Shui practitioners.

The biggest concern of traditional practitioners is that much of the tradition, philosophy, theories, and rich history of Feng Shui are lost in translation. Some regard the departure from tradition in New Age as a blatant lack of honor and respect. They argue that, without proper consideration, the new idea only creates more confusion and misunderstandings.

Regardless of which system of Feng Shui you use, bear in mind the heart of Feng Shui lies in the study and observation of Qi – so let's explore that concept now.

chapter 4

UNIVERSAL QI: THE LIFE FORCE OF FENG SHUI

"Qi rides and scatters with the wind, and collects at the boundaries of water." – GUO PO'S "THE BOOK OF BURIAL" (CIRCA 300 A.D.)

FIGURE 2: CHINESE CHARACTER FOR *QI*.

Qi – pronounced "chee" (and often seen spelled as "Chi" in the West) – translates into English as "energy." It is one of the most important concepts in Feng Shui.

Qi governs all things in the universe. It is an ever-present force that is in a constant state of flow, circulating and permeating in and around you everywhere. Indeed, it connects all living things – the human body, nature and the changing of the four seasons, the stars above, the Earth, and the Sun.

In simple terms, Qi is just the flow of energy. It is a natural, dynamic occurrence that feeds and creates life. Without it, there is no life.

This abstract energy is not visible to you and me, of course, but it is manifested in everything you see, touch, smell, feel, and hear. (I'll give you an example in a moment.)

Although individual Qi has its unique composition and quality – growing, expanding, retreating, or passive – you are connected to and influenced by it, no matter its form. This is why Qi is the core essence of the practice of Feng Shui. The energy of your environment and surroundings directly impact you, your mind and body, your house's fortune, your relationship with other family members, your luck cycle, and your personal endeavors. This is a notion many people intuitively "get," but not always at first. I encourage you to stay with it and keep grappling with the existence of Qi.

You can find the concept of Qi in many cultures. Vedantic philosophy, Hindu religion, and the practice of yoga, for example, refer to Qi as *prana*. In the West, it is called *life force* or *vital energy*.

Although it may remain a mystery to people who need to <u>see</u> to <u>believe</u>, the idea of Qi is in everything, and it's the key to accessing the world around you. It is the underlying foundation, or gateway, to understanding your relationship with your environment, body, mind, other people, and all living creatures.

For instance, Western astrology analyzes how the movements and positions of the planets will affect you energetically; Acupuncture and Ayurveda medically diagnose and treat sickness by identifying energy blockages or imbalances in the body; and scientific experiments continue to prove the powerful existence of energy, not just among living creatures, but also in space.

That's where Feng Shui comes in!

The goal of Feng Shui is to harness the naturally occurring cosmic energies from your environment – yes, Qi – to bring positive influences to your life's endeavors.

THE SCIENCE BEHIND QI

Science helps us understand the natural laws present in the universe.

Take the Earth and the Sun. As the Earth orbits the Sun, science has proven that there is an astrological effect, or star-pull effect, that stimulates the energies in the space around them, thereby affecting and influencing all living things on Earth.

Many renowned scientists agree that there is a dynamic oscillation form that connects everything and links every living being in the universe. Everything is energy, so they refer to this phenomenon as "vibration," meaning everything vibrates. Because every living creature is made up of unique particles (or Elements, in Chinese Metaphysics), you also emit a certain frequency or vibration.

Vibration also has an official scientific name: electromagnetism. The science behind electromagnetism is complex, but the application is quite straightforward. "Electro" is the output, and "magnetic" is the input. With this newfound understanding, you can begin to associate everything as having an "in" and "out."

Here's that example of how Qi actually manifests itself.

When you drop a pebble in a pond, you see the ringlets moving outwards, and under the surface of the water, the rings eventually return inward – to the exact same spot where the pebble was dropped. This also explains why when you go about your day in a good mood, good things tend to happen to you. You are emitting a kind of vibrational energy waves, so you attract the same kind of vibrational energy waves back to you. What you put out, you get back. This gives another layer of understanding to why energy, albeit intangible, is cyclical and always in motion. This is also the Law of Attraction: Like attracts like.

QI AS A LIVING ENTITY – IN THE MIND, BODY, AND ENVIRONMENT

Qi flows in and around you in a current, like electricity. It is an invisible, yet ubiquitous, force. You cannot see it, of course, but you can certainly see manifestations of it around you – in nature, in the environment, in your home, and in your body.

Anatomically speaking, energy is necessary for living things to survive. Human beings, for example, acquire energy from food, along with oxygen and the energies from the natural environment. When your body is nurtured with vital energy, your overall wellbeing – physical, psychological, and emotional – is healthy. Therefore, evaluating how the abstract energy of your space is moving is an important role of Feng Shui.

In Feng Shui, we identify the patterns of Qi.

All Qi patterns, whether retaining or dissipating, affect all aspects of the human experience: your wealth, career, relationships, health, and spiritual cultivation. These aspects also represent your personal unique "fortune" that is directly impacted by the Qi patterns of your environment.

Feng Shui practitioners assess and evaluate Qi quality in order to achieve a desired outcome. A good practitioner has a solid understanding of how to redirect, revitalize, refresh, slow down, or speed up the energy to support the space and the people.

Important note: Although Qi can be gathered artificially in a certain area with manmade objects such as sharp angles, poison arrows, and bow-shaped roads, be mindful that energy is a natural, cosmic phenomenon. We cannot produce more. In the traditional practice of Feng Shui, Qi must be derived and assessed from the environment. As Albert Einstein once said, "Energy cannot be created or destroyed. It can only be changed from one form to another."

....
THE FIVE BODIES OF QI
You will be exploring many types and qualities of Qi throughout this book. Before you delve deeper into the workings of Qi in Feng Shui, here you will see there are five primary bodies of Qi. The ability to decipher these different bodies of Qi is an important step to understanding how this life force in your environment will affect you.

We categorize Qi bodies as having five distinct properties:

Prosperous Qi

This is considered the strongest kind of Qi quality. Imagine a bell curve graph. The highest tip of the curve is representative of Prosperous Qi. It is the optimal flow and most positive type of Qi.

Growing Qi

This body of Qi is traditionally referred to as "Sheng Qi," and it is the kind of energy that possesses life-generating qualities. Growing Qi is more conducive to positively supporting new efforts, such as a new career, project, or business venture. In a bell curve graph, the Qi movement is upward, ascending toward Prosperous Qi.

Retreating Qi

This type of Qi is slowing down, losing its power and momentum, and moving into a downward slope. The strength of this Qi is still acceptable, but it won't be strong enough to benefit new endeavors or to sustain current efforts.

Dead Qi

This is also called stagnant or stale Qi. This type of Qi has no movement at all. It simply collects and sits without influence. Because it has no effects, Dead Qi is not considered positive.

Killing Qi

This type of Qi is also called "Sha Qi" and possesses harmful qualities because, unlike Dead Qi, Sha Qi is still active and moving. It is considered the most unfavorable kind of Qi. It must be avoided or deflected. If this Qi is present and influencing an important aspect of one's life, it can create disharmony, conflict, and even physical injury and misfortune.

chapter 5

Chinese Metaphysics Explained

> *"Everything should be made as simple as possible... but not simpler."*
> — ALBERT EINSTEIN

Chinese Metaphysics is part of Taoism, a philosophy based on Qi energy, the principles of Yin and Yang, and the theory of The Five Elements.

In your quest to learn the true derivation of Feng Shui and the role it plays in the wide spectrum of Chinese Metaphysics, it's important to understand just two concepts: the Five Arts and the Cosmic Trinity. Here's a quick rundown. I think you'll be fascinated by how it all fits together.

THE FIVE ARTS

The Ancient Chinese divided Chinese Metaphysics into five distinct categories:

Mountain Art is referred to as Philosophical Art, because students and practitioners are immersed in the teachings of Confucianism and Taoism, which govern the mind and awareness. It is also the study of mental and physical longevity. The idea there is to cultivate good health through diet, meditation, and pugilistic exercises such as Tai Chi or Qi Gong. This art promotes longevity of the body and mind by moving the Qi in the body from the inside to the outside.

Medicine Art refers to all forms of Traditional Chinese Medicine (TCM) – acupressure, acupuncture, herb medicine, pulse reading, and mental or spiritual therapy. This practice focuses on identifying and unblocking energy flows by way of interconnected pathways throughout the body called "meridians." This art differs from its counterpart, Mountain Art, in that the goal is to move the Qi from the outside in.

Divination Art is also called the Art of Prediction. It is based on the universal wisdom of the Yi Jing (or I Ching), one of the earliest Chinese classic texts. There are several different techniques, including the early divination practice of the Yarrow Stalk, Plum Blossom Oracle, and casting of the Three Coins called King Wen's Oracle System. The skill of the practitioner lies in his or her ability to accurately interpret the message derived from one of the 64 Hexagrams, each representing a particular life situation or circumstance. The aim of the practice is to provide a means for one to understand the choices before them.

Destiny Art is the study of a person's life luck and destiny. Practitioners use BaZi, often referred to as The Four Pillars of Destiny, to systematically and logically analyze personal birth charts. That analysis provides a greater understanding about yourself, including your talents, strengths, and weaknesses. It also predicts the ups and downs of your luck cycle throughout life. Purple Star Astrology is also included in this study. *Note: BaZi is often used in tandem with the practice of Classical Feng Shui.*

Physiognomy Art is the study or observation of appearances. The original intent of the practice requires the practitioner to carefully observe the natural formations of the environment in order to assess the quality of Qi. Therefore, the practices of Feng Shui, Face Reading, and Palm Reading are all part of Physiognomy Art.

NOTE FROM JEN: *As you can see from the explanation of The Five Arts, Feng Shui is one of five components that make up the science of Chinese Metaphysics as a whole.*

THE COSMIC TRINITY

According to the ancient classics, there are three distinct – but interconnected – forces that influence your journey in life. Each one is equally weighted in importance without regard to hierarchy or order. The Cosmic Trinity, also called the Power of Three, is made up three types of luck:

Heaven Luck, or Destiny Luck, refers to your destiny DNA. It is believed that, at the instant of your conception, you captured the energy of the universe at that moment in time. It cannot be changed. In other words, Chinese Metaphysics teaches that one-third of your life's path may be predetermined by destiny. These factors include the timing and location of your birth, who your ancestors are, the circumstances you were born into, your family background, and your innate talents and limitations. These are the things that "fate" or "destiny" predetermined for you. This is your ultimate purpose in life and it is unique to each and every person.

Man Luck refers to the things you <u>can</u> control. This, of course, is free will. These are the choices you make every day to improve (or worsen) your life. These include your virtues, actions or inactions, decisions, behaviors, emotions, attitude, thoughts, education, cultural and religious beliefs, and the people you choose to associate with. You ultimately decide how you want to see and experience each stage of your life's path, and how you will successfully navigate each obstacle and grow from it.

Earth Luck refers to the influences of your environment and how the energy in the environment interacts with your personal energy. These influences come from the spaces you occupy in your home, as well as the places you choose to work, spend time in, and raise your family. Practitioners use and apply Feng Shui to harness the benevolent energy from the earth to positively influence your life.

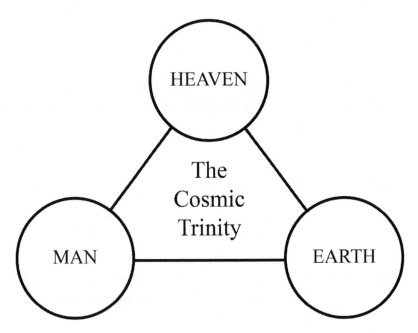

FIGURE 3: THE COSMIC TRINITY DIAGRAM.

NOTE FROM JEN: *If you follow the concept of the Cosmic Trinity, the impression that Feng Shui is "magic" or a "cure all" becomes unsustainable. The philosophy of the Cosmic Trinity states that your destiny is governed equally by three separate but unified forces. Feng Shui can play a big role but can only ever influence one-third of your life's journey through Earth Luck. To change the outcome of your destiny, the Chinese believe you must first have good ancestral luck (Heaven), have good virtues to increase your personal luck (Man), and then implement good Feng Shui (Earth).*

chapter 6

YIN AND YANG: THE HARMONIC DANCE

> *"Happiness is not a matter of intensity but of balance, order, rhythm, and harmony."* — THOMAS MERTON

The Yin and Yang image is one of the most famous symbols in the history of the world. People in almost every culture and nation on earth can name it, and they recognize it immediately as signifying balance and duality.

Let's talk about the profound meaning behind this symbol and its long, rich history. You'll see why it plays an important role in the practice of Feng Shui.

THE BEGINNINGS OF YIN AND YANG

When the Chinese first identified Qi as the universal life force thousands of years ago, they noted that Qi is formed by a partnership of dual polar opposites. However, this is not about two opposed forces clashing. Think of it as two extremes working together and complementing each other. In the same way magnets have a north pole and a south pole, and atoms have positive and negative forces, Qi has both Yin and Yang qualities.

The nature of Yin and Yang lies in the interdependence of two extreme energies constantly at play – changing, moving, and interacting – without ever entering a permanent state of stillness. The harmonic dance of Yin and Yang is literally an exchange of energy – one exerting, the other receiving. It is this continuous and dynamic circular motion of force that nourishes every living creature.

But let's step back a moment.

To understand the derivation of Yin and Yang, you've got to start with the concept of Wu Ji.

Wu Ji translates to mean "The Great Void" or "The Grand Ultimate." The idea is that in the beginning, before there was life and existence, the universe was a vast space of nothingness and void. And so, this story is first depicted by the image of an empty circle.

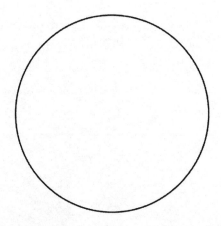

FIGURE 4: WU JI – THE GRAND ULTIMATE.

At some point thereafter, some unexplainable event triggered the moment of "realization." This is also referred to as awareness or consciousness. This first moment of awareness marked the beginning of existence. This phenomenon, called the Tai Ji (or "The Great Limit within the Unlimited") is represented by a single dot in the center of the empty circle.

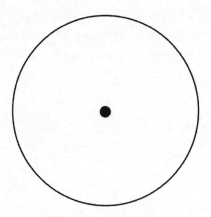

FIGURE 5: TAI JI – THE GREAT LIMIT WITHIN THE UNLIMITED.

From this newfound enlightenment, the Yin and Yang energies – the two sides to everything – were born.

The symbolic image of Yin and Yang is often depicted by two halves. The authentic image shows the white half (sitting on the left, slightly above) as representing Yang. The black half (sitting on the right, slightly below) represents Yin. The halves are separated – not by a straight, sharp line but by a soft, curved line, like two fish bodies merging into each other.

FIGURE 6: YIN AND YANG SYMBOL.

But there's something else, too. As you can see from the image above, within the white Yang there is a black dot, and within the black Yin there is a white dot. This symbolizes that there are always two sides to everything. The two sides, albeit opposites, are always complementary, and always striving for balance. It is the ultimate representation that there is always Yin within the Yang and Yang within the Yin.

TWO SIDES TO EVERYTHING

When you grasp this concept, you can begin to appreciate the many dualities (or pairs) all around you in nature.

Here is a poignant piece written by Taoist philosopher Lao Tzu, describing this very idea.

"All the world knows beauty
but if that becomes beauty
this becomes ugly
all the world knows good
but if that becomes good
this becomes bad
have and have not create each other
hard and easy produce each other
long and short shape each other
high and low complete each other
note and noise accompany each other
first and last follow each other."

The physical manifestations of the Yin and Yang concept can easily be found in the partnerships of the world: female and male, small and big, short and tall, soft and hard, passive and active. Everything has two parts. And so the circle of Yin and Yang is the foundation of every identity in the universe.

When you further dissect the dual forces of life and nature, you can appreciate the stunning revelation that humanity (or the human experience) cannot exist solely on one side, or on one thing.

Here's an excellent example: nature's gift of dawn and dusk. At both times, the day and night shift effortlessly and naturally from one into the other, like a dance. It begs the question: Can you experience the night without the day and the day without night? Because it is in that one perfect moment – as the sun rises or sets – that you fully experience the coming-together of two forces, in unison and in perfect harmony.

This is true of everything in life.

In essence, every phenomenon or natural occurrence in the universe is derived from the interaction between the dual forces of Yin and Yang.

Without one extreme, can you truly appreciate the opposite?

Can you know joy without pain? Happiness without suffering? Warmth without coolness? Light without darkness? Woman without man? Softness without hardness? Birth without death? These are all part of nature's dual chromosomes. They all rely on each other and simply cannot exist – at least not fully – without the other.

Here's an example of how Yin and Yang interplay to define ideas:

Yin	Yang
Dark	Light
Night	Day
Black	White
Female	Male
Round	Sharp
Soft	Hard
Small	Large
Moon	Sun
Cool	Warm
Death	Birth
Passive	Active
Rest	Movement
Cold	Hot
Wet	Dry
Slow	Fast
Earth	Heaven
Sleep	Work
Quiet	Loud

Again, though, the theory of duality does not suggest a dialogue of opposites clashing. It suggests the harmonic unity of two extremes coming together.

As the English saying goes, "opposites attract." The existence of one keeps the other "in check." They both become their best – whatever they are – because of the existence and presence of the opposite. Too much of anything creates discord and imbalance and prevents the natural flow. Yin and Yang is the epitome of "seeking" balance. One side is exerting just enough for the other to blend and balance in response – not replacing but merely accommodating – in one single reality.

In Feng Shui, Yin and Yang provide us with the framework to work with the Qi from your environment to support the abstract energies of your home. Yin is associated with the mountain – enclosed and quiet. Yang is water – active, open space. Hence, the location where the mountain ends is where water begins, which is the point or place where you will find the concentration of Qi – the connection between Yin and Yang. This is also called the "Dragon's Den."

As such, the workings of Yin and Yang in Feng Shui allow you to achieve that near-perfect balance and harmony, like "a match made in Heaven."

NOTE FROM JEN: *Be careful that you do not interpret Yin and Yang as a "thing." Instead, it is the* **relationship** *between the two sides of everything that makes it Yin and Yang. For instance, female by itself is not Yin, and male itself is not Yang. Instead, it is the relationship* <u>between</u> *female and male that make them Yin and Yang.*

chapter 7

THE FIVE ELEMENTS: NATURE'S GIFT

> *"If people do not revere the Law of Nature, it will inexorably and adversely affect them. If they accept it with knowledge and reverence, it will accommodate them with balance and harmony."* – LAO TZU

In traditional Taoist view, everything – solid or abstract – can be classified into five basic elements: Wood, Fire, Earth, Metal, and Water. Their basic qualities and modes of interactions are used to understand virtually everything that happens in the universe, from the rise and fall of empires and the workings of internal organs and human emotions (Traditional Chinese Medicine), to the very passage of time.

As you'll see, they're vital to the practice of Feng Shui.

THE FIVE ELEMENTS IN CHINESE METAPHYSICS

The Chinese have long observed the cycles of nature. They revered and admired the gifts of the seasons as nature progresses through its unending cycle. And they believed human beings experience the same cycles of change within.

Maybe you've noticed this in yourself. As the seasons shift, your physical nature – mind, body, emotions – reflects these changes.

Think for a moment about the clothes you wear, the foods you eat, your mood, and the cycles of thought and emotion that arise in you with the start of a new season.

As the leaves begin to turn and fall in the autumn, you prepare to let go of the workings of the hyperactive mind and begin to slow down. You gradually pile on the layers and witness the obvious shifts of the changing colors in your surroundings. In the winter, you cocoon and nest and reach for heavier, heartier foods to warm up your body. As spring approaches, your senses are stimulated and reawakened. The flowers bloom, grasses become green, and everything comes alive again, signifying a new beginning. And when you arrive at the peak of summertime, you shed any remaining layers kept from seasons past and bask in the heat and sunshine, overwhelming the body with aliveness and movement.

You become the season. And so you are the elements.

Because you are a member of nature, nature invariably lives inside you. For this reason, the need to balance nature's elements inside yourself and your home is an important component in the practice of Feng Shui (if not the most essential). The elements guide you to reach that near-perfect Yin and Yang state that creates the harmonious flow in your environment to support your body and endeavors.

••

WOOD, FIRE, EARTH, METAL, WATER

The concept of the Five Elements is the driving force that brings about change. It activates and moves the energy in all aspects of life. It resides in your organs, emotions, thoughts, values, actions, preferences, and behaviors. It is manifested in the seasons and directions. It can be assigned a number, a color, a scent, or even a musical note. The elements are universal and they exist in everything.

Let's explore the nature and characteristics of each one.

Wood

Description: Visualize a simple tree. It is the true embodiment of life. While you can't witness the entire cycle of a tree spurting up from a seed and growing into a 30-foot-tall plant in a single flash, you do realize it is growing. It matures in a slow yet persistent state. If it gets adequate nourishment with water and sunlight and care, the tree grows consistently and steadily, upward and outward into a beautiful, strong, living being.

Looking at the bottom of the tree, you can see its tenacious roots, firmly gripping and embracing the earth beneath it. Moving slowly upward, you observe its impressively thick, powerful body – the trunk full of history that it has carried throughout the seasons. The branches flow outward with gentle magnificence as they ride with the wind… while flexible and bending, they are robust and sturdy. The lush green of its leaves emits vibrancy and health.

At its strongest, the tree can have the persistence and stubbornness of a weed and the power to move earth with its roots. At its gentlest, the tree dances in the wind, celebrating the joys of rebirth. Regardless of how harsh or accommodating the seasons may be, the tree remains upright. It's determined to stay rooted in place for as long as it can stand.

People are much the same. When we get what we need from nature, we flourish. And when we are flourishing, we expand, grow, and live.

Movement: The Qi movement for Wood is expansive in all directions.

Qi Representation: Energetically, the Wood element represents growth, life, expansion, durability, resilience and determination, intuition, creativity and imagination, flexibility, benevolence, and health.

Imbalanced Qi: When Wood energy is imbalanced, you may experience stagnant growth, a creative block, stubbornness, or literally feel off balance, as if you have lost your footing.

Physical Manifestations:

- Things physically made out of wood
- Colors green, blue-green, teal
- Plants and flowers

Fire
Description: A fire of any size is a powerful and lively force. A body of fire together exudes warmth and light to everything around it. Looking directly at the fire, you see a form that is full of spark and vibrancy. It charms and mesmerizes you into a hypnotic state. You cling to its every move, watching the flames waltz with the wind… it flickers and moves in all directions, elegantly flowing in no particular pattern.

What will it do next? Will it rage into a fiery blaze and overwhelm you with its heat and power? Or will it comfort you with warmth and grace?

The amazing form of Fire never stays static in color. Just when you think you have reached a moment of oneness and understanding with it, it teases you by changing from red to orange to yellow. It may even surprise you with an unexpected moment of purplish-red. What a dynamic sight!

The burning glow commands respect. It demands that you acknowledge it, feel its presence, and admire its greatness.

Fire has a strong association with the human heart. When it's fed by the wood's healthy quality of benevolence, creativity, and inspiration, the heart grows with passion and joy. The core of a person's heart is thereby fueled with sincerity and pure love.

Movement: The Qi movement for Fire is upward.

Qi Representation: Energetically, the Fire element represents passion, assertiveness, leadership, healthy emotional interactions with people, and radiance.

Imbalanced Qi: When the Fire energy is imbalanced, you may experience lack of motivation or passion, coolness, aggression, agitated tension, impulsiveness, or short-temperedness.

Physical Manifestations:

- Colors red, orange, pink, purple-red
- People and animals (including images of people and animals)
- Items that give heat and light (candles, light bulbs)

Earth

Description: Earth is the ground beneath your feet. It is the foundation you build your home on and live on. Earth also grows the food that nourishes and cultivates the mind and body. Its soil is rich, fertile, and dense, supplying a solid base to plant your feet firmly so that you feel safe, stable, nourished, and grounded.

Earth is often depicted as the center of all movements, because it represents the effortless transition between the seasons in a steady and constant state. Seasonally, it represents late summer, when the days are still infused with the warmth of summer, but the golden light of autumn is approaching. It is a time of ripening and harvesting.

Life forms on the earth's surface exist primarily by consent of nature's partnership with the heat from the sun (fire) and the nutrients from the rocks, formed from the burning and erosion of lava deposits. Scientifically, volcanic rocks are known to make some of the best soils on earth. They are abundantly rich and fertile, so lush vegetation grows in them.

You can always count on the earth to play its part. After all, it is the mother and provider of all life – the pillar of balance and security.

Movement: The Qi movement for Earth is horizontal, spinning horizontally in the same direction as the earth's axis.

Qi Representation: Energetically, the Earth element represents satisfaction, sensuality, calmness, fertility, stability, centeredness, and harmony.

Imbalanced Qi: When the Earth energy is imbalanced, you may feel heavy, lethargic, overweight, unfulfilled, stuck, anxious, insecure, overly conservative, and self-centered.

Physical Manifestations:

- Earth-tone colors, such as yellow, beige, terra cotta, tan, and brown
- Items made from pottery or clay
- Images of the earth, such as peaks, valleys, fields, meadows, plains, and canyons

Metal

Description: Metal is probably the toughest element to experience directly in nature. In most cases, Metal is seen as cold, hard, sharp, and even destructive, yet the element has an essential role in nature.

Metal is representative of the minerals from the earth. These substances, extracted from the ground you stand on, provide so much of what is needed to sustain life – fuel for heat, materials for structural strength, and gems for beauty.

Another thing that makes the Metal element unique from the other elements is its "low key" nature, efficiently performing and executing its magnificent duties behind the scenes. It is powerful yet inconspicuous.

The Metal element is often used for structural support, representative again of its magnitude and power. Buildings, houses, roads, highways, and bridges are all reinforced and bolstered by Metal. The wires we use in systems of communication (such as your telephone, computer, and television) and transportation are also examples of the workings of Metal. It gives substance for communities to build networks and helps ensure all things are functioning properly. It is the key ingredient that holds things together.

On the other hand, Metal also embodies beauty as seen through the charm and elegance of the jewels extracted from the rich soil of Mother Earth. Such precious treasures!

Characteristically, the natural element of Metal also epitomizes the righteousness of a person – justice, loyalty, uprightness, integrity, virtue, devotion, and strength.

Movement: The Qi movement for Metal is condensing and contracting, but can also move in a sharp, piercing motion.

Qi Representation: Energetically, the Metal element represents altruism, loyalty, decisiveness, independence, endurance, and intelligence.

Imbalanced Qi: When the Metal energy is imbalanced, you may be indecisive, judgmental, and unable to reason clearly. You may lack logic or come off as abrasive or cold.

Physical Manifestations:

- Colors white, silver, gold, metallic and other shiny colors
- Items made out of metal, such as stainless steel, brass, copper, silver, and gold

Water

Description: Looking at a body of water, you notice it always takes the shape of the object that holds it. Its abstract form is dynamic and fluid, always flowing, forceful and sentimental all at once. The imagery of water is soothing and comforting, like the sea journey, the search for the fountain of youth, and the picture of the old watering hole.

The Yin and Yang synergy of Water is clearly observed, from its massive forms like the ocean, to its gentle nature like a drop of mountain dew. In many ways, Water is life, an essential component to preserving and sustaining life. When you come in contact with Water, either by drinking or bathing in it, you feel invigorated and refreshed, along with the sensation of being "washed over" with clarity, awareness, inspiration, and wisdom. The experience is both cleansing and detoxifying!

Anatomically speaking, you and I are both of the Water element – 78% of the human body is composed of it. Similarly, you have within you the ponds, rivers, reservoirs, seas, and oceans of the Water energy – the sources of life. It drives you to seek meaning and purpose, to transform fear to hope and optimism, restore brilliance, and cultivate vision.

Water is the lifeline and gateway to all parts of life, not just in nature, but also in the human body and spirit. The energetic ebb and flow drives the dynamic changes that are the essence of life.

Movement: The Qi movement for Water is downward and descending.

Qi Representation: Energetically, the Water element represents intelligence, wisdom, adaptability, fluidity, perception, brilliance, faith, and spirituality.

Imbalanced Qi: When the Water energy is imbalanced, you may feel anxious, fearful, stressed, wishy-washy, and unable to commit.

Physical Manifestations:

- Things that are black, dark, or gray
- Images and objects of water features, such as a pool, water fountain, lakes, ponds, and aquariums

NOTE FROM JEN: *Understanding the Five Elements means going deeper than the physical manifestation of the elements itself. The elements also embody a type of Qi and can represent a myriad of attributes. Depending on the circumstances of the Feng Shui analysis, different attributes will be used to properly* *assess the overall Qi of the space and residents to see how it affects the physical and the abstract.*

THE RELATIONSHIP CYCLES: PRODUCING, WEAKENING, AND CONTROLLING

To understand how the elements interact with each other in nature, you will explore three basic laws that govern the relationships between them. The cycle of relationships are called Producing, Weakening, and Controlling.

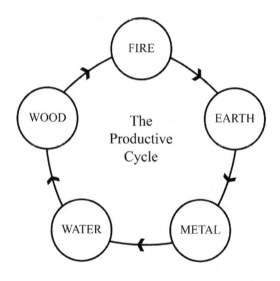

FIGURE 7: PRODUCTIVE CYCLE.

Productive Cycle

The Productive Cycle (often referred to as the Nourishing Cycle or Cycle of Birth) is straightforward. In the normal cycle of nature, each element "feeds" each other, producing strength or energy for the other to grow and flourish. Think of this as one element giving *birth* to the other, like a mother to a child.

The Productive Cycle is generally viewed as a harmonious relationship among the elements and flows in a clockwise direction. The easiest way to remember this cycle is to follow the normal cycle of nature:

- Wood burning generates Fire
- Fire burns to ashes and creates Earth
- The Earth's soil is mined for Metal
- Metal contains Water (or Metal melts like Water)
- Water nourishes and grows Wood

Weakening Cycle

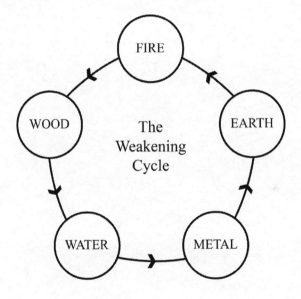

FIGURE 8: WEAKENING CYCLE.

The Weakening Cycle is also called the Reductive Cycle. It runs in a counter-clockwise direction, or backwards from the Productive Cycle. When one element is nourishing and supporting the other, the self-element is naturally weakened – like one sacrificing itself to give strength or energy to another.

Follow this scenario:

- Wood is weakened when burnt by Fire
- Fire is weakened when diminished by Earth
- Earth is weakened when Metal is mined and extracted
- Metal is weakened when melted to produce Water
- Water is weakened when absorbed by Wood

Controlling Cycle

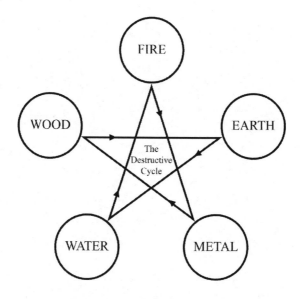

FIGURE 9: CONTROLLING CYCLE.

The Controlling Cycle (also called The Destructive Cycle) moves in a star-like direction. As its name conveys, each element exists to also control, subjugate, or destroy another in order to retain some form of equilibrium. This relationship cycle is considered the most aggressive kind. It can often disturb or aggravate the other elements if it is not assessed properly.

Follow this scenario:

- Wood penetrates Earth
- Fire melts Metal
- Earth dampens Water
- Metal cuts Wood
- Water extinguishes Fire

NOTE FROM JEN: *If you are starting out in Feng Shui, I highly recommend that you refrain from using the Controlling Cycle. Remember, the aim of the theory is to bring BALANCE. Without formal training, using the Controlling Cycle may aggravate or generate additional imbalances. If you must soften an element that is too strong, consider using the Weakening Cycle to harmonize and balance the energies in your environment.*

chapter 8

THE FOUNDATIONAL TOOLS OF YOUR FENG SHUI WORK

> *"I can't change the direction of the wind, but I can adjust my sails to always reach my destination."* — JIMMY DEAN

This chapter is, by its very nature, a compact introduction to the whole subject of Classical Feng Shui. If you're new to Feng Shui, it will be a particularly important one to understand (along with the principles of the Five Elements and Yin and Yang).

The concepts outlined here are the fundamental basics of the workings of the authentic practice, especially when you begin to apply various techniques like Flying Star Feng Shui. These theories may not be obvious to you at first, but allow the ideas to sink in as you explore them. We will be revisiting these concepts throughout the book.

As for those who are already practicing, I hope this section serves as a useful refresher.

. . . .

BA GUA

Ba Gua literally translates to "Eight Trigrams" in English. *Ba* means "eight" and *Gua* means "trigram."

This is an important component of Chinese Metaphysics that symbolizes the natural phenomenon and forces of nature, especially in Feng Shui and I Ching Divination. It is also used in Taoist cosmology to represent the fundamental principles of reality.

The Eight Trigrams was supposedly discovered by Fu Xi (2852-2737 B.C.). He was considered the father of many things. He was a prominent figure of his time, a sage ruler, and a cultural hero who left behind a very important legacy. In the classical Chinese text "Baihu Tongyi" (written by Ban Gu), Fu Xi's discovery of the Eight Trigrams is summarized in this way:

> "In the beginning there was as yet no moral or social order. Men knew their mothers only, not their fathers. When hungry, they searched for food; when satisfied, they threw away the remnants. They devoured their food hide and hair, drank the blood, and clad themselves in skins and rushes. Then came Fu Xi and looked upward and contemplated the images in the heavens, and looked downward and contemplated

the occurrences on earth. He united man and wife, regulated the fives stages of change, and laid down the laws of humanity. He devised the eight trigrams in order to gain mastery over the world."

Drawn from the concept of the Tai Ji (or Yin and Yang), the trigrams are viewed as a universal symbol of balance and harmony. Even though the trigrams appear simple at first glance, the meanings behind them are deep. They contain great wisdom and valuable clues regarding the abstract forces that affect man on earth.

Individually, a single trigram can mean a million different things, including a family member, a number, an animal, a body part, an element, human personality, or a compass direction. Collectively, the Eight Trigrams describe how nature works. They provide a means for human beings to better understand how to live a naturally balanced life within themselves and their environment.

NOTE FROM JEN: *The 64 Hexagrams (a set of six lines) used in I Ching Divination was derived from the original formation of the Eight Trigrams.*

How Are the Trigrams Formed?
A trigram is composed of three horizontal lines and formed from the bottom up (similar to how a house is constructed from the earth up – you don't start by building the roof!). Therefore, when constructing the trigrams, always start at the bottom.

The top line represents heaven. The middle line represents man. The bottom line represents earth. They are the three forces that govern all existence, similar to the idea of the Cosmic Trinity in Chapter 5.

A single line can be represented by either a solid or broken line. A solid line (——) denotes Yang, and a broken line (– –) is Yin.

The Eight Trigrams can be divided into four distinct groups: Greater Yang, Lesser Yang, Greater Yin, and Lesser Yin. Let's walk through how the groups are formed.

When a single solid line is stacked above another solid line, this is called **Greater Yang** (two Yang lines).

——————

——————

When you place a Yang line above a Yin line, this is called **Lesser Yang**.

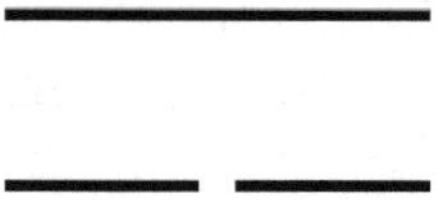

——————

———   ———

When a single broken line is stacked above another broken line, this is called **Greater Yin** (two Yin lines).

———   ———

———   ———

When you place a Yin line above a Yang line, this is called **Lesser Yin**.

———   ———

——————

Why are these groups significant?

These four images represent the inevitable stages (or cycles) of nature: birth, growth, decay, and death. They also show the continuous changing of the four seasons – from spring to summer to autumn to winter. And from these four images, you can add a third line at the top, alternating between a Yin and a Yang line, to form the Eight Trigrams. Taoist philosopher Lao Tzu once referenced the trigrams as such:

"The Tao gives birth to one
one gives birth to two
two gives birth to three
three gives birth to ten thousand things
ten thousand things with *yin* at their backs
yang in their embrace
and breath between for harmony."

NOTE FROM JEN: *"Ten thousand things" is a Chinese saying that means "everything."*

From the Greater Yang, you have Qian (乾) and Dui (兑).

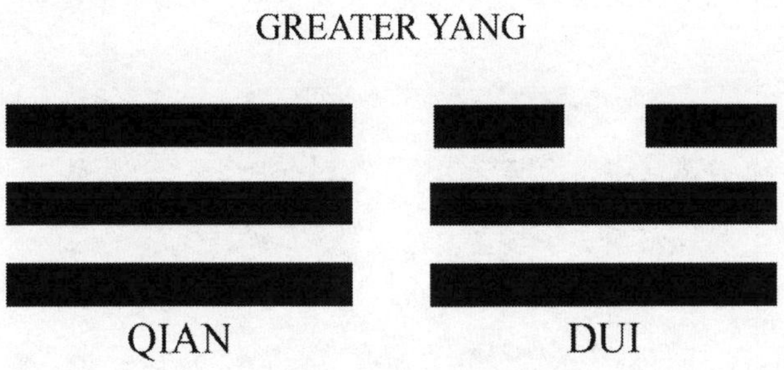

GREATER YANG

QIAN   DUI

FIGURE 10: QIAN AND DUI.

From the Lesser Yang, you have Kan (坎) and Xun (巽).

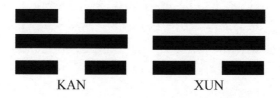

FIGURE 11: KAN AND XUN.

From the Greater Yin, you have Kun (坤) and Gen (艮).

FIGURE 12: KUN AND GEN.

From the Lesser Yin, you have Li (离) and Zhen (震).

FIGURE 13: LI AND ZHEN.

NOTE FROM JEN: *The Eight Trigrams is also a binary code, similar to the coding languages used to program computers. Fascinating, isn't it?*

What Do the Trigram Symbols Mean?

Ba Gua helps us understand everything in the universe, giving human beings the wisdom and insight to lead their lives according to the way of the cosmos. The table below briefly summarizes some key attributes most commonly used in Feng Shui.

Name	Nature	Direction	Element	Number	Family Member
Qian 乾	Heaven	NW	Metal	6	Father
Kan 坎	Water	N	Water	1	Middle Son
Gen 艮	Mountain	NE	Earth	8	Youngest Son
Zhen 震	Thunder	E	Wood	3	Eldest Son
Xun 巽	Wind	SE	Wood	4	Eldest Daughter
Li 离	Fire	S	Fire	9	Middle Daughter
Kun 坤	Earth	SW	Earth	2	Mother
Dui 兑	Lake	W	Metal	7	Youngest Daughter

NOTE FROM JEN: *You'll notice there's no number 5 in this table. That's because 5 is the connector between all the rest of the numbers. I'll explain why and how this works in just a few pages, when we talk about the Ho Tu!*

We will revisit this table later in the book, because these attributes are important references used in the application of Flying Star Feng Shui (in Chapter 13). The trigrams and their associated numbers are also related to the numbers seen in the Luo Shu chart discussed below.

The Early Heaven Ba Gua Arrangement

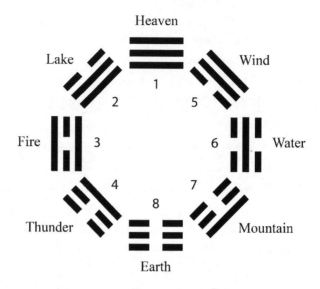

FIGURE 14: EARLY HEAVEN BA GUA ARRANGEMENT.

The figure above is known as the Early Heaven Ba Gua. It was Fu Xi's original formation of the Eight Trigrams circa 2800 B.C.

Legend has it that Fu Xi arranged the trigrams according to the landscape of China by placing Heaven on the top, in the south (in the past, the direction of south was located at the top in Chinese maps), and Earth at the bottom, in the north. Fire trigram is in the east to represent the rising of the Sun, and Water trigram is in the west to represent the Moon. The other four trigrams are placed in the corners, with Mountain trigram in the northwest, Lake trigram in the southeast, Wind trigram in the southeast, and Thunder trigram in the northeast.

This arrangement is considered a "perfect" model of harmony and balance because the trigrams are formed in contrary pairs (i.e., Yin and Yang), depicting the most natural and ideal state of life (in permanent stillness).

Another way to remember how the Early Heaven Ba Gua is arranged is that the trigrams are organized based on opposing forces or balancing complementary pairs of opposites. It also represents the "innate" energy force that was <u>originally created</u>, where there is no movement or passage of time.

NOTE FROM JEN: *The Early Heaven Ba Gua arrangement is believed to carry the power of protection. As such, the symbol is often found in Chinese homes, hung as a "Ba Gua Mirror." Although this object is often associated with Feng Shui, the Ba Gua Mirror is more a superstition or cultural icon rather than a genuine Feng Shui object.*

The Later Heaven Ba Gua Arrangement

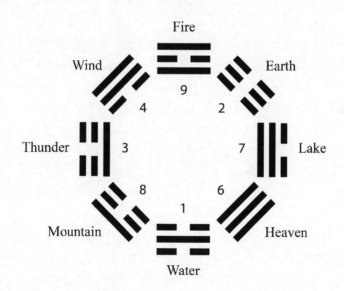

FIGURE 15: LATER HEAVEN BA GUA ARRANGEMENT.

Real life, of course, is not static. So the dynamic movement of time (or the constant changes in life) is reflected in a subsequent arrangement known as the Later Heaven Ba Gua. King Wen rearranged the Eight Trigrams according to the changes of the Five Elements in the four seasons. He was a famous ruler during the Zhou Dynasty (1027-221 B.C.) and was credited with discovering the 64 Hexagrams in I Ching Divination.

To reflect the true nature of life and the ways of the universe, King Wen placed Fire trigram (summer) in the south, Water trigram (winter) in the north, Thunder and Wind trigrams (spring) in the East and Southeast, respectively, to represent spring, Lake and Heaven trigrams (autumn) in the west and northwest, respectively, to represent autumn, and Earth and Mountain trigrams (late summer) in the southwest and northeast, respectively.

This subsequent arrangement is an important evolution. The Later Heaven Ba Gua truly depicts the emergence of the human experience, the dynamic flow of energy, and the ever-changing movement of the environment. That stands in stark contrast to the Early Heaven Ba Gua, which shows the ideal state of life if there were no changes and no movements. Therefore, the easiest way to remember the Later Heaven Ba Gua arrangement is that the trigrams are organized based on the cyclical nature of the world; the focus is achieving balance by accepting change and the passage of time.

Since the Later Heaven Ba Gua reflects the real world we live in today, this arrangement is the one all Feng Shui students should attempt to learn and master.

NOTE FROM JEN: *The concept of the Ba Gua appears in many cultures and societies, including the Flag of South Korea (the Taeguk Flag), which has the image of the Ba Gua. Singapore's one-dollar coin is shaped like a Ba Gua* *(octagon). The Flag of South Vietnam has a trigram representing "south." The Taoist martial arts form called Taijiquan uses the principles of the Ba Gua in its movements, as well.*

LUO SHU

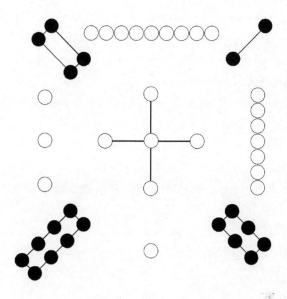

FIGURE 16: THE LUO SHU DIAGRAM.

The fundamentals that govern the thoughts and applications of Classical Feng Shui must include a discussion of the Luo Shu. It is one of the most ancient Feng Shui tools. The study always comes back to this important emblem.

Luo Shu (also called The Magic Square) is one of two mathematical diagrams that is said to represent the energies of the universe. The other diagram is the Ho Tu (which we'll get to shortly).

The Luo Shu is a mathematical wonder (and the concept is adapted in many ancient cultures) and is essentially like program coding for software. It is the driver that dictates how Qi is calculated. It incorporates the factors of the eight cardinal and intermediate directions, the Five Elements and their Yin and Yang variations, the four seasons, time, and Qi properties in a single chart.

Because Qi is a dynamic phenomenon, the Luo Shu chart represents the <u>directional flow</u> of Qi within a property.

Where the Luo Shu Came From

The origin of the Luo Shu is an extraordinary story. It goes like this. A wise man saw a tortoise emerge from the water near the River Luo in China around 2205 B.C. The man noticed the strange dot-like markings on the back of the shell of a tortoise and soon realized that the round dots represented the numerical patterns of the natural rhythm (or the law of nature).

NOTE FROM JEN: *Many historians and scholars claim that the wise man was Emperor Yu (2205-2197 B.C.).*

FIGURE 17: THE TORTOISE EMERGING FROM THE RIVER LUO. IMAGE COURTESY OF RAYMOND LO.

How to Read the Luo Shu Chart

4	9	2
3	5	7
8	1	6

FIGURE 18: THE LUO SHU CHART BASE MODEL (IN NUMBERS).

Let's break down the components piece by piece. Firstly, the Luo Shu chart above shows a three-by-three grid composed of nine squares (also called "Palaces"). Each grid contains a specific integer from 1 to 9 (also called "Stars") in their original and fixed positions. The four even numbers reside in the corners, and the odd numbers form a cross in the center.

When you add the three numbers in each row or column – horizontally, vertically, and diagonally – the total always equals 15, which is the number of days in each of the 24 cycles of the Chinese Solar Year. It is also the number of days in the cycle of the New Moon and the Full Moon.

The direction of south is always marked at the top, with north at the bottom. The path always begins with the number 5 in the center, and moves according to the directional sectors, which are always fixed.

To illustrate, the flow of Qi always begins with number 5 in the center, then moves to the northwest (6), west (7), northeast (8), south (9), north (1), southwest (2), east (3), and finally stopping at southeast (4).

The direction described above, in essence, is called the "Luo Shu Path," and it establishes the dynamic movement of energy in a property according to the Five Elements, the natural progression of the four seasons, and the passing of time.

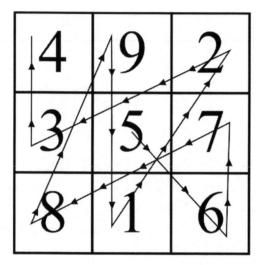

FIGURE 19: DIRECTIONAL FLOW OF QI (OR LUO SHU PATH) AS SHOWN IN THE LUO SHU CHART.

The picture above is only meant to illustrate the fundamentals of the base model of the Luo Shu chart. In practice, the chart may not necessarily show the static location of each Palace number in a single location, especially in Flying Star Feng Shui. For example, Eight Mansion Feng Shui uses the original base model of the Luo Shu chart (as shown in Figure 18 above). On the other hand, Flying Star Feng Shui recognizes that the numbers in the Luo Shu chart are not "frozen" in place. Because Flying Star observes the dynamic movement of energies, the numbers do not stay in place permanently either (like they do in Eight Mansion). The Luo Shu Path, however, will always move the same way, regardless of where the numbers land.

An example is illustrated below. Notice how the number 8 resides in the center Palace where the numbers have shifted, but the directional movement of the Luo Shu Path remains the same.

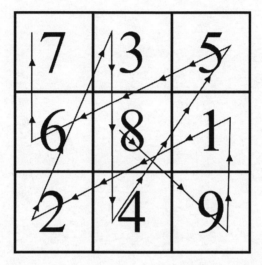

FIGURE 20: DIRECTIONAL FLOW OF QI AS SHOWN IN THE LUO SHU CHART WITH STAR 8 IN THE CENTER.

NOTE FROM JEN: *The book "The Language of Numbers Demystified" by Robert Dickter describes how the Chinese used the higher orders of the Luo Shu chart for astronomical purposes to represent some kind of language to yield pertinent information about time, space, and the cosmos.*

In addition, Jacob Bronowski's 13-part series documentary, "The Ascent of Man," gives a fascinating introduction to how the Chinese revered these mathematical models. It suggests that perhaps the ancient people were familiar with the Pythagorean Theorem, long before Pythagoras himself came around. The fact that the Pythagorean Theorem presents itself in the Luo Shu format demonstrates that the arrangement of numbers is a form of communication, connected with algebra, and could generate sacred numbers, such as the numbers of the calendars.

HO TU

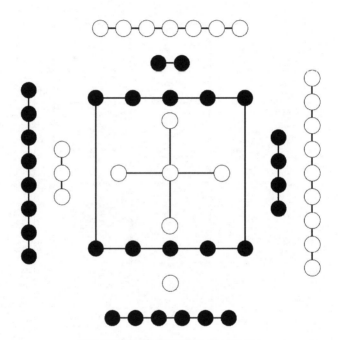

FIGURE 21: THE HO TU DIAGRAM.

Where the Ho Tu Came From

The Ho Tu is also referred to as the "Yellow River Map" and is the second most important mathematical base model in Feng Shui. The Ho Tu markings were discovered near the Yellow River during the Hsia Dynasty (2150-1557 B.C.) on a beautiful white horse. Except this was no ordinary horse. Often called the "Fire Horse," the mythical creature had the body of a horse and the head of a dragon. And on its body, it bore dot-like markings similar to the Luo Shu diagram on the tortoise.

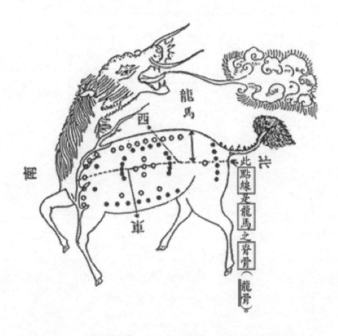

FIGURE 22: FIRE HORSE EMERGING FROM THE YELLOW RIVER. IMAGE COURTESY OF RAYMOND LO.

Ancient sages noted that the markings on the Fire Horse contained the static, or the absolute perfect, state of Yin and Yang. While the Luo Shu chart depicts the dynamic movement of the universe, the Ho Tu, on the other hand, depicts the most ideal state (or utopia) where there is no movement, change, or evolution.

How to Read the Ho Tu

Although the Ho Tu numbers are embedded in the Luo Shu, the Ho Tu numbers are different. They are shown in pairs as having a relationship, versus a single number influence like those found in the Luo Shu.

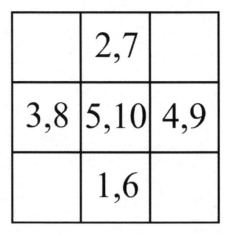

FIGURE 23: THE HO TU DIAGRAM (IN NUMBERS).

In the combination of the Ho Tu, the number 5 is the pivotal connector. Within the nine numbers, there are four pair combinations. To illustrate, 1 plus 5 is 6, therefore 1 and 6 is a pair; 2 plus 5 is 7, therefore 2 and 7 is a second pair; 3 plus 5 is 8, therefore 3 and 8 is another pair; finally, 4 plus 5 is 9, therefore 4 and 9 represent the final pair.

The diagram below demonstrates how the Ho Tu numbers were derived from the Luo Shu.

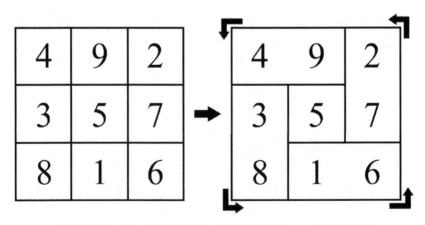

FIGURE 24: LUO SHU CHART CHANGED TO HO TU CHART.

The Ho Tu numbers can also be assigned a specific compass direction and an Element:

- Numbers 1 and 6 reside in the North and represent the Water element.
- Numbers 2 and 7 reside in the South and represent the Fire element.
- Numbers 3 and 8 reside in the East and represent the Wood element.
- Numbers 4 and 9 reside in the West and represent the Metal element.

In addition to the four pairs above, 5 and 10 is the fifth pair, representing the Earth energy residing in the Center.

You'll also notice that the combinations are always represented by both an even (Yin) number and an odd (Yang) number.

In Flying Star Feng Shui, we put a lot of emphasis on the Luo Shu diagram; however, the Ho Tu is equally as important and compelling, especially when applying advanced theories and application from the San Yuan school. I will exclude the advanced-level discussion of Ho Tu combinations to stay true to the introductory materials in this book.

NOTE FROM JEN: *The takeaway for you here is that the Ba Gua, Luo Shu, and Ho Tu formations provide the forces behind the development of many Feng Shui formulas and techniques.*

In Grand Master Raymond Lo's practitioner book, "Feng Shui Essentials," he describes the Ho Tu diagram as the birth cycle of the Five Elements, while the Luo Shu is its counterpart, representing the cycle of destruction. In essence, the two mathematical models are the balancing forces in the universe.

LUO PAN

NOTE FROM JEN: *In this next section, I'm not going to teach you how to use a Luo Pan. That's a whole book unto itself! Instead, I'm going to give you a general introduction on WHAT it is and WHY it is used in Classical Feng Shui. If you are interested in diving more into the workings of a Luo Pan, Stephen Skinner has a great book called "Guide to the Feng Shui Compass."*

All Classical Feng Shui practitioners operate a traditional magnetic compass called the Luo Pan. Luo means "Everything," and Pan means "a Bowl." This can be interpreted as the compass being a device to unravel the ambiguities of a space and allegorically refer to the union of Heaven and Earth, and specifically everything else that holds all matters together.

Legend has it that the Yellow Emperor was fighting the mythical creature known as Chi You during the Battle of the Zhuolu around 2500 B.C. When the Yellow Emperor and his army became trapped in a thick fog and were near defeat, the Heaven sent a woman to his aid. This woman, the patron deity of the divination arts, is known only as the Goddess of the Nine Heavens. She presented him with a charm that was a south-pointing magnetic needle. The Yellow Emperor placed this needle at the front of his chariot that eventually navigated him out of the fog, subsequently defeating the enemy, and winning the battle!

While this story is quite amazing, this event became a pivotal and significant turning point in the history of Feng Shui, and the Yellow Emperor is credited as having invented the first Feng Shui Compass.

Thereafter, Classical Feng Shui considers the Luo Pan as an essential tool (and in many ways, it is also considered a divination tool) designed with specific bearings and markings to enable the practitioner to take accurate directional measurements of a property or an object in the environment. In this way, Qi can be properly assessed based on location and direction of the subject.

The Luo Pan is regarded as a specialty compass. You can appreciate the intricacy of its design and intention just by looking at it. An average Luo Pan contains anywhere from 3,000 to as many as 6,000 characters! They include many different markings, symbols, numbers, yin-yang, 64 Hexagram, the Early Heaven Ba Gua arrangement, and Chinese characters for various formulas and techniques, such as 24 Mountains, 72 Dragons, Great Sun Formula, 120 Gold Divisions, and 28 Constellations, to name a few.

Using the Luo Pan in Classical Feng Shui is like having a racket to play tennis or a paintbrush to paint. It is a must-have tool in order to do a proper Feng Shui assessment.

How Does the Luo Pan Work?

Traditionally, there are two types of compasses: The San He Luo Pan and The San Yuan Luo Pan. If you recall, these are the two Compass School systems described in Chapter 3.

In recent times, a third compass was developed to accommodate practitioners who practice both the San He and San Yuan systems. Below is a San Yuan San He combined compass designed by Grand Master Raymond Lo.

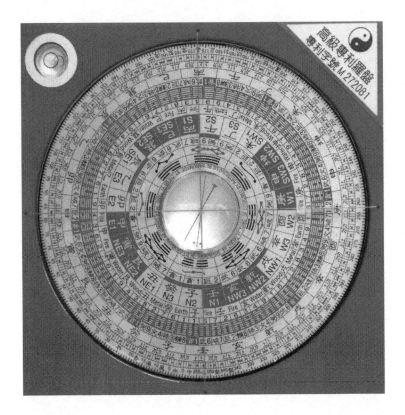

FIGURE 25: RAYMOND LO SAN YUAN SAN HE COMBINED LUO PAN.

Regardless of which compass you use, all of them are different from a conventional compass. One of the most obvious differences is its north-finder. A Luo Pan is a magnetic compass that depicts Magnetic North as opposed to True North (or North Pole of Earth as shown by GPS or electronic compasses).

The aesthetics of the Luo Pan also set it apart from conventional compasses. Every Luo Pan has either a metal or wooden plate, known as the "Heaven Dial" or "Heaven's Pool." The term refers to the center of the Luo Pan that contains the compass needle. The circular metal or wooden plate typically sits on a wooden base known as the "Earth Plate." This enables the Heaven Dial to rotate freely on top of the Earth Plate. Two red wire or nylon threads are placed on top like a cross. They serve as the pointer to note the position on the ring of a subject or structure. It also has a "spirit level" in one corner of the Earth Plate to ensure the compass is being held level.

Traditionally, the square base of the compass is red, too. That symbolizes good fortune in Chinese culture. Red is also said to have a strong protective color to keep energies clear around the device.

Another important distinction about the Luo Pan is that it counts 24 directions instead of the traditional eight cardinal and intermediate directions (north, east, south, west, northeast, southeast, southwest, and northwest). How? The Luo Pan takes each one and divides it further into three sub-directions. As such, a Luo Pan will delineate the traditional direction as 1, 2, or 3. For example, north 1, north 2, north 3, northeast 1, northeast 2, northeast 3, west 1, west 2, west 3, and so forth.

The 24 directions, also more popularly known as "24 Mountains," are significant because each "ring" or direction on the Luo Pan represents one single Feng Shui formula, along with a Yin or Yang quality. Since a whole circle is 360°, precise measurements can be taken in as little as 15° intervals (360 ÷ 24). This method enables the practitioner to take very precise measurements of the direction of the property. For example, a conventional compass will point south at 180°, whereas a Luo Pan will show south as a 45° between 157.5° and 202.5°.

The significance of these directions correlates with how the Five Elements flow in and around a property. Practitioners use them to identify any changes or adjustments that need to be made to attract and promote positive Qi.

Luo Pan in Feng Shui Assessments

A Luo Pan is the only way to get an accurate reading of the facing and sitting directions of a property, because this reading is the underlying formula for all of the analyses that follow.

A responsible practitioner should take multiple readings, especially when there are magnetic interferences, to ensure accuracy. Automobiles and building structures can cause problems. Creating an analysis based on inaccurate readings is worse than doing nothing to correct or remedy the inauspicious or unfavorable elements in your home. This is why all Feng Shui professionals must receive adequate and proper training, as well as practical experience, in order to conduct a directional reading and perform an accurate Feng Shui assessment.

chapter 9

CLASSICAL FENG SHUI:
THE FOUR IMPORTANT FACTORS

"You will know you have found your home when both your physical environment and energetic surroundings are in harmony with the individual you are within." — MADISYN TAYLOR

Classical Feng Shui is the study of Qi that focuses on four important factors that influence the space you inhabit. They are the environment, property, time, and people. In this chapter, we're going to explore each one.

ENVIRONMENT

Classical Feng Shui is a "macro" practice because it first focuses on what is happening <u>outside</u> the property. In order to take advantage of the optimal flow of nature's prosperous energy, you cannot ignore the influences of the external environment. Where you choose to build a home, for instance, plays an important role on how Qi will affect your life.

During an assessment, a practitioner will first examine the external features surrounding the property. In Feng Shui, the environment refers to the natural landforms of nearby mountains, the slopes and curvatures of the land, the design of nearby water formations, and where they are situated in relation to the property. This also includes man-made constructions, like roads and highways and neighboring buildings, including the assessment of the Four Celestial Animals (which we will explore in Chapter 10). All of these landscapes and structures stimulate the circulation and flow of Qi. Therefore, it is vital to properly assess what is around the property in order to understand how Qi is moving and behaving within the area.

Remember, the goal of Feng Shui is to tap into the positive flow of natural Qi and bring that inside your home. Harnessing "good" Qi must therefore start with your environment, because what surrounds your home is far more important than the structure, aesthetics, or interior. Any formations of inauspicious landforms will adversely affect the Qi quality (or fortune) of your home, and no amount of Feng Shui "cures" will remedy this.

PROPERTY (SHAPE, FACING DIRECTION, MAIN DOOR)

Properties and other structural buildings are often viewed as "containers" of Qi, meaning the space within a property holds energy, both favorable and unfavorable.

To do a Feng Shui assessment, you must also consider the following external features before assessing the Qi flow of the property's internal space:

- The property's shape,
- The property's facing direction, and
- The location of the property's Main Door

Shape

When you are looking at the shape of a building or house, you are assigning its shape to one of the Five Elements to determine whether the property is supported (or weakened) by its immediate surroundings.

Let's say you are assessing a property that has a rooftop that is prominently shaped like a triangle. According to the Five Elements doctrine, the triangular shape of the house most likely belongs to the Fire element.

FIGURE 26: A HOUSE WITH A TRIANGLE ROOFTOP (FIRE ELEMENT).

On the other hand, if the property's neighboring homes have a flatter rooftop shaped like a cube, then these homes most likely belong to the Earth element.

FIGURE 27: A HOUSE WITH A FLAT ROOFTOP (EARTH ELEMENT).

If this is the case, the Five Element cycle of birth indicates that Fire produces Earth, giving Earth strength, while the self-element of Fire is weakened.

Of course, you should assess the external Feng Shui of the property in its entirety. However, with this simple observation, you can preliminarily conclude by saying that the fortune of the property under assessment (with the triangular-shaped rooftop) is weakened, rather than supported, by its surroundings.

How do you interpret this finding as it relates to the occupants? Because the fortune of the home is weakened at the front of the property, the house is already tapping into weak Qi; therefore, the residence may experience some loss of wealth and success.

The example described above is a very simplified illustration. I am merely making a textbook reference. In practice, the significance of the evaluation of the external shape of a property can be quite complex, and the severity of the influence – good or bad – must also be tailored specifically to each property and its unique internal Qi components. Furthermore, this evaluation extends not only to the physical shape of the building itself, but also to the shape of the plot of land on which the property stands.

When you take an aerial shot of a property and its surrounding, for instance, you can visualize the shape or cut of the land from a higher perspective. This enables you to also evaluate the physical structure of the land properly. Is it balanced, stable, and smooth? Or is it jagged or jutting – factors that do not generally facilitate the proper flow of Qi? In addition, this kind of analysis provides a wider scope for an environmental assessment that is the root of the advanced practice of Forms School Feng Shui.

Facing Direction

Identifying the orientation of a property is an important step in performing an accurate Feng Shui assessment, because it will dictate how Qi flows in and around the building and serve as a reference point for all subsequent computations.

The most common mistake people make is assuming the property's facing direction is the same as the property's Main Door. This is not necessarily true. In some cases, the Main Door to the building is on a different side from the primary facing direction of the building. The façade of the building is often designed to have a "facing" view, whether that is a lake, a pond, the entryway of the subdivision, a garden, a road, or some other scenery. Therefore, the Main Door may or may not always be located on the same side.

The key is to follow the original architectural design of the property, rather than the direction or location of the Main Door.

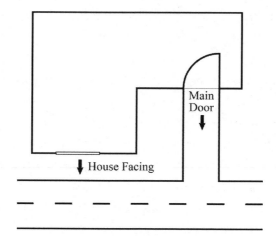

FIGURE 28: MAIN DOOR IS LOCATED ON THE SAME SIDE AS THE PROPERTY'S FACING DIRECTION.

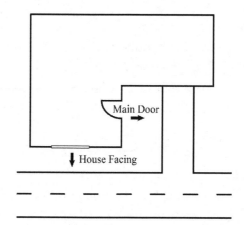

FIGURE 29: MAIN DOOR IS LOCATED ON A DIFFERENT SIDE THAN THE PROPERTY'S FACING DIRECTION.

Some properties with more complex and modern architectural designs will require experience and judgment in order to conclude what the property's facing direction is. Moreover, this is a basic but very important skill and it takes proper training and practice to master.

Main Door

Locating the property's Main Door relates to the assessment of the "Bright Hall." The Bright Hall of any property is usually an open space that facilitates the gathering of Qi before it enters the property. The open space promotes the flow of positive Qi by allowing it to collect, gather, and settle before entering and influencing the interior space. We'll explore this concept in more detail in Chapter 10.

TIME

Because time is the force that captures the essence of change, it cannot be overlooked or downplayed. In fact, time is an important variable in assessing the Qi quality of the environment and the driving force in interpreting how Qi behaves and affects the spaces in which you live.

While some of you may perceive change as a scary and ambiguous thing, in Chinese Metaphysics, change is accepted as a kind of gift to humanity. As a matter of fact, change is the fundamental means by which you grow and evolve. And it is inevitable no matter how much you may resist it.

And so, change is often experienced as the passing of time. The most obvious manifestation is the changing of the seasons. Because everything in the universe is interconnected, you are invariably part of change. And this extends to everything else around you – your environment, your body, relationships, moods, dreams, and even the way you respond to the shifts in the energetic qualities in your space.

Because Qi and the factor of time go hand in hand in Feng Shui, Qi pattern is assessed as it relates to the changing of the time. Time is not static (because of change). The energy quality surrounding your environment is also not static. The dynamic force of Qi flow is literally moving and flowing in a constant and cyclical state.

Ever wonder why a particular house may have been so beneficial or prosperous in some years, only to witness its fortune deteriorate in the next? When you understand that fortune, luck, or energy is not permanent (again, due to change), it makes sense.

To help you understand the cyclical divide of time, in Classical Feng Shui, time is demarcated into a mathematical calculation. It is said that in 2637 B.C., the Yellow Emperor invented a time counting system referred to as the Three Periods and Nine Ages.

Here's how it works.

This mathematical system operates with the assumption that there are three "periods" of time, and each of the three periods spans 60 years. Therefore, one cycle is 180 years. The origin of 180 years is unclear, however, it has been debated that the time counting system relates to the fact that every 180 years, all of the planets in the solar system are in alignment.

The three "periods" are called Upper Period, Middle Period, and Lower Period. When you sub-divide the 60 years again by three, you will have a time span of 20 years. Every 20 years is also called an "age."

The diagram below shows the current Three Periods and Nine Ages:

A Cycle (180 Years)		
Upper Period	**Middle Period**	**Lower Period**
Age 1 (1864-1883)	Age 4 (1924-1943)	Age 7 (1984-2003)
Age 2 (1884-1903)	Age 5 (1944-1963)	Age 8 (2004-2023)
Age 3 (1904-1923)	Age 6 (1964-1983)	Age 9 (2024-2043)

This time system started in 2637 B.C. when it was first invented, and has been running continuously until today. From the table above, the start date of the current Cycle was February 4, 1864; however, there is no specific significance either dynastically or in terms of the Christian or Western Gregorian calendar. Also, the table shows the Cycle will end in February 2044. It does not mean the end of the world! This simply means that, in the context of the Chinese calendar, it is the end of the 25th Grand Cycle (of 180 years). The next Cycle, or the 26th Grand Cycle, will begin all over again. As you can see, the Chinese have had accurate calendars a lot longer than the West.

At the time of this writing in 2013, we are at Age 8 (2004-2023).

With time constantly changing, shifting, and moving, the dynamic influences of Qi occurs every hour, every day, every month, and every year. However, the intensity and force of these influences are part of a much larger shift in an age (every 20 years), in a period (every 60 years), and in a cycle (every 180 years).

· · · · · · · · · · · ·
PEOPLE
In Classical Feng Shui, individual qualities, characteristics, talents, and needs are honored.

The practice recognizes that as a result of individual differences, as well as different elemental compositions of the person, people will generally respond differently to the influences of the Qi qualities in their environment. So the same space may result in different outcomes for different people. As such, we always consider "the people factor" when assessing the Feng Shui of a property.

It is not uncommon for a Classical Feng Shui practitioner to gather certain personal information about the residents during a consultation. The most common one is birth data – year, month, day, and time of birth. This enables the practitioner to not only understand your elemental make-up, but also to use the information to examine the dynamic relationships among the family members in the household (or a team of staff if you are doing a business consultation), as well as to direct how and where to scrutinize the Feng Shui challenges of the property.

chapter 10

CLASSICAL FENG SHUI: THE ESSENCE OF EXTERNAL FORMS

> *"Look deep into nature, and then you will understand everything better."*
> – ALBERT EINSTEIN

In Chapter 2, I mentioned a book called "The Book of Burial." The author, Guo Po, was a natural historian, philosopher, and prolific writer of his time. His book is considered an important ancient text because it was the first document to ever talk about Feng Shui.

In his writing, Guo Po pointedly articulated what "good" Feng Shui is in one famous sentence: "Qi rides and scatters with the wind, and collects at the boundaries of water." Many serious Classical Feng Shui professionals have this line very well memorized!

There are two important references in this sentence: wind and water.

Because Qi is an invisible force, it's difficult to picture. Guo Po gave us two reference points when examining the landscape of the environment. In the natural movement of Qi, it is carried and moved by the wind and scattered across the land. Without anything stopping or "catching" the wind, Qi cannot be collected to nurture the land. That's why mountain and water formations became very important features to scrutinize when assessing the Qi quality of the environment – they "collect" Qi, like a wall "collects" snowdrifts.

To apply Forms Feng Shui in the modern times, you pay attention to everything that has an influence on how Qi is emanated in the external environment. Not only are you looking for the physical presence of nearby mountains and water, but you are also looking at the buildings, colors, and shapes of objects; the contours of the neighborhood; the location of manmade infrastructure, such as roads and freeways; the shapes of the plot of land the buildings stand on; and anything else that has an appearance and is visible to the naked eye.

This is the core practice of Forms Feng Shui.

To simplify an otherwise very complex and advance application, let's focus on the basics of mountain and water formations. These two are the fundamental factors when examining and assessing the environment using Forms Feng Shui.

NOTE FROM JEN: *While Guo Po's book defines Feng Shui based on the landscape for Yin Houses, many of the concepts highlighted are also useful in classifying the external features for Yang Houses. Remember, Yang House* *represents dwellings for people, and Yin House represents burial sites for the dead.*

MOUNTAIN FORMATIONS

Mountains are grand and impressive. They exude a majestic quality. Physically, they have defined slopes on both sides and a much higher elevation as compared to their surrounding landforms.

To really appreciate the formidable presence of mountains, you need a basic understanding of how they are formed.

Geologically, there are several ways mountains are created. In one particular way, the earth's tectonic plates crash together. Because of the tremendous power – or energies – involved, the sides of the plates crumple in an explosive collision, forcing the land to jut upwards. Although they crash with colossal force, the formation process takes millions of years!

This natural occurrence is an important external phenomenon that is observed and appreciated in Classical Feng Shui.

When mountains are demarcated in terms of Qi quality, they are considered "Yin" because of their immobility and stability and shelter-like quality.

In Forms Feng Shui, mountains are called "Dragons of the Land" or "Energy of the Dragon." In this case, the Dragon refers to a range of mountains surrounding a property. Why the dragon? A traditional Chinese dragon looks like a snake or a serpent. The body is long and winding and moves up and down. Therefore, in Feng Shui, the term Dragon describes mountain ranges that have a lot of variation in altitude and span a long distance.

FIGURE 30: A TRADITIONAL CHINESE DRAGON.

When you observe nearby mountain formations, there are several things to consider in order to determine what kind of Qi they are emitting. It's all to do with their physical appearance. Is it green and lush, signifying health and life? Or is it barren, jagged, and rocky, generating negative Qi? What about its shape? Which element does it belong to and how does it support its surroundings?

FIGURE 31: A PICTURESQUE MOUNTAIN RANGE.

Where the mountains are located in relation to your property provides more vital information for evaluating the Qi quality of the environment. Generally speaking, you want to see healthy mountain ranges situated <u>behind</u> a property. Because mountains are considered Yin (stable and immobile), having mountains behind a home is seen as a good thing, providing a sense of security and support for it and promoting positive relationships and good health to those who occupy the space.

Mountains also act as shelter against strong and violent winds. Ranges formed around a property in an "embrace" are regarded as more advantageous, because this type of formation provides protection and a curvature to catch or stop the wind (or Qi) from escaping. In Forms Feng Shui, where the wind stops, the energy stays put. Therefore, the places where energy is concentrated will be considered most auspicious.

FIGURE 32: HEALTHY MOUNTAIN RANGES
SUPPORTING THE BACK OF A PROPERTY.

NOTE FROM JEN: *In Forms Feng Shui, man-made objects, such as houses and buildings, are also considered mountain formations.*

THE FOUR CELESTIAL ANIMALS

Long before the Feng Shui compass was developed, Feng Shui practitioners were also skilled astronomers. They assessed the Qi in the environment by observing the clusters of stars in the heaven and the contours of the land on earth.

As I explained when we talked about the Five Arts in Chapter 5, Feng Shui is the study of the landscape's appearance. To understand how the abstract energies are influencing an area, you must first examine the natural formations of the land surrounding the property. This method is considered to be the original and oldest technique.

Generally speaking, when a property is said to have "good" forms, it is implied that it was built on land that is "embraced" by the proper positioning of the Four Animals, which we'll explore below. Such a conclusion is important because it means the landforms surrounding the property are conducive to allowing energy to generate, circulate, and flow naturally, externally and around it.

This is an important step in Classical Feng Shui because, if the goal is to harness positive Qi to support your internal space and endeavors, what better source than your external environment?

People mistake Feng Shui as being only about the internal aesthetics of the property's design and décor. While the beauty of your internal space plays a factor in the human psyche, this thought is an incomplete one. In Classical Feng Shui, if a property is built on land that does not adequately support it with positive Qi, then it is said that the fortune of the house is already weak.

How do we assess the favorable formation of the land surrounding the property?

In Classical Feng Shui, the Four Celestial Animals provides a means to evaluate and measure your external environment in relation to the property you inhabit. It is also used to locate the best placement of your home (if you were to scout for land to build on). Unfortunately, with land becoming scarcer, and most homes built in urban developments and subdivisions, it's become more difficult to apply the concept of Forms Feng Shui.

Nonetheless, don't overlook the principles of Forms Feng Shui, regardless of the type or circumstances of property, because Qi in the environment is always influencing and affecting the whole set-up.

In Forms Feng Shui, a home that is surrounded by positive Qi should have the Four Celestial Animals at each of the four main compass directions (north, east, south, west) outside of the home, embracing the home.

The Four Celestial Animals are referred to as Black Tortoise, Green Dragon, White Tiger, and Red Phoenix. They sound mythical, I know, but the names are simply derived from the shapes or clusters of the star constellations, making it easier to memorize and reference them.

Black Tortoise
The Black Tortoise represents the mountain form that sits behind the property, facing north. Ideally, the mountain should be higher than the property to provide strong protection, support, and stability to the home and those living in the home.

Green Dragon
The Green Dragon references what is on the left side of the house (when viewed from the Main Door looking out). The Green Dragon represents springtime and brings wealth and prosperity to the home. In Forms Feng Shui, this is represented by a low hill, mountain, or neighboring property to the east of the property where the sun rises.

The Green Dragon essentially provides a makeshift "embrace" around the side of the property, protecting it from violent Qi.

White Tiger

Like the Green Dragon concept, the White Tiger references what is on the right side of the house facing out – or west of the house where the sun sets. The White Tiger embrace ensures that whatever Qi is collected does not escape. A low hill or mountain to the right of the house secures and prevents positive Qi from leaving the area.

Red Phoenix

The Red Phoenix references what is at the front of the house facing out – or the south side of the property toward the Sun. The Red Phoenix brings fame, special recognition, and new opportunities to the residents of the home.

Red Phoenix is also commonly referred to as "Table Mountain" formation. This is translated to mean that when you are standing in front of the Main Door of the property looking out, you see the mountain form from a distance. If the height of the mountain is at eye or shoulder height, then it is said that the property has good Table Mountain to "lock in" the Qi and prevent good Qi from leaking away.

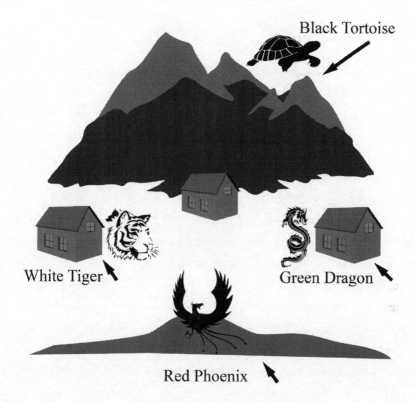

FIGURE 33: THE FOUR CELESTIAL ANIMALS SURROUNDING A PROPERTY.

NOTE FROM JEN: *Please don't interpret the Four Celestial Animals to mean you should buy animal figurines to enhance the external environment of the property! (I've seen this – seriously.) Remember, the animal names merely reference the shape it takes from the constellations above, and are used to help us understand how to evaluate the environment easily. The Art of Physiognomy is about natural physical landforms, not man-made figurines!*

WATER FORMATIONS

Water is an essential resource to life, like food and oxygen. Seventy percent of the Earth's surface is water, and we are blessed with a myriad of beautiful water formations everywhere, from stunning glaciers and roaring waterfalls to lakes and ponds. They are cool and serene, also majestic by their own design.

Some parts of the world will naturally enjoy more bodies of physical water than others (i.e., Florida versus Arizona). While it may seem more difficult to identify the physical location of water formations than mountains, water is actually all around you; you just have to know how to find it.

For instance, man-made objects like roads and freeways are also considered water formations, because they have comparable energy to the flow of the river. When the traffic is stronger and heavier, the flow of the river is stronger. And because of the active motion of the flow of traffic, this stimulates the Qi in the area.

In Forms Feng Shui, water formation is called "Blood of the Dragon" or "Dragon's Blood," and it produces "Yang" Qi because of its dynamic and ever-moving nature. It ebbs and flows with the current – backwards and forward, fast and slow – always taking the shape of the things that hold it. Therefore, water formations are generally ideal in front of the property, supporting the Main Door entrance.

When it comes to assessing the Qi quality in front of the house, there are three basic ways water moves around a property.

1. Towards the house,
2. Away from the house, and
3. Crossing in front of the house.

Water Moving Towards the House

A Water formation that comes directly towards the house creates a motion that promotes a rush of energy that is too strong. Think of a house that sits on a T-junction road facing the straight road ahead. The direct line of the house's Main Door with the T-junction road creates a force that gushes toward you in an aggressive manner (versus a soft, sentimental, and meandering motion). This Qi quality is referred to as "Sha Qi," or Poison Arrow.

NOTE FROM JEN: *The Poison Arrow must be in direct line with the property's Main Door or windows; otherwise, there are no negative effects.*

FIGURE 34: MAIN DOOR FACING A T-JUNCTION ROAD.

Water Moving Away from the House

While mountain energy is associated with people and health, water energy is associated with money and fortune. Therefore, the least favorable kind of water formation is one that *moves away from* the house, suggesting that money and fortune for the residents will also slip away.

FIGURE 35: WATER FORMATION MOVING AWAY FROM THE HOUSE.

You may also have a water formation that bypasses the house, like a house that sits on a Y-junction. While the water has a forward motion coming towards the house, the flow motion is "turning away," completely missing the house. This is not a favorable Forms feature, either.

FIGURE 36: A HOUSE SITTING ON A Y-JUNCTION ROAD.

Water Crossing in Front of the House

A road in front of a house or an office building is common. It's the case in most metropolitan cities. Think back to Guo Po's famous line of wind and water, which says a straight-across water formation is not conducive for Qi to stay put – it merely moves from one place to the next. If the flow of traffic is heavy, such as a highway or freeway situated in front of the house, then this external feature is not considered positive. The flow of energy is moving too fast to be useful to the house.

FIGURE 37: BUILDINGS FACING A BUSY FREEWAY.

NOTE FROM JEN: *There are no negative effects for a house that sits in front of a normal residential street where cars can stop and park freely.*

WATER FORMATION SCENARIOS

So what's the most ideal water formation? Much like the embrace of mountain ranges around the backside of the house, you want to have a similar embrace of water features in the front and around the front side of the house.

The most obvious solution is to not have any negative Forms to start with. However, in modern times, this is often unavoidable. Most architectural designs of homes and roads today do pose a Feng Shui challenge. They are often constructed in an angular shape with sharp edges, like a rectangle.

While these external features may not always be the "perfect" Feng Shui, it is important to take heart that these features do not necessarily make or break a house's fortune.

Feng Shui is meant to be a practical application that offers flexibility to the circumstances. Furthermore, the influences of the dynamic energy (such as Flying Star) must also be evaluated in order to assess the severity of these negative external forms and how they may positively or negatively affect the internal forms.

We will continue to explore these two ideas throughout the book. For now, let's have a look at some common water formation examples that pose a Feng Shui challenge, and how to address them.

Scenario 1: Water moving towards the house (T-junction example).

Solution: To minimize the aggressive rush of energy hitting a house straight on, you can create a blockage. That slows it down. Since Poison Arrow is considered a Wood element, you can use the landscape by planting trees and bushes, such as a round floral garden (Metal), around the front side of the house. That blocks the direct hit and neutralizes the Wood energy. While you do not want to block the water Qi completely, you can strategically redirect and "round" the flow before Qi enters the Main Door.

If changing the landscape is not practical, one common cure suggested by Classical Feng Shui practitioners and masters is to place two Kirin as guards at the Main Door – one on each side. Otherwise, implementing items in Red (Fire) such as a red door or a red-colored doormat will also help calm the strong Wood energy.

NOTE FROM JEN: *Kirin is a legendary animal commonly used in traditional Classical Feng Shui practice. It has the head of a dragon, horns of an antelope, the scale body of a fish, the tail of an ox, and the four legs and hooves of a deer. They usually come in pairs and are known for their protective nature against negative energy making its way inside the home.*

Scenario 2: Water crossing directly in front of the house.

Solution: There are several solutions for this type of challenge. The first is to create a structural design that looks like "arms" of the house, like a U-shaped embrace. This can be done by creating an extension from the side of the house, either with a wall, fence, or foliage. You can also achieve this by creating one arm (instead of two), like an L-shape in the opposite direction of the flow of traffic.

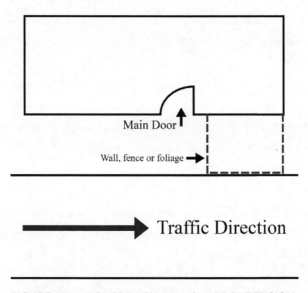

FIGURE 38: A HOUSE WITH AN L-SHAPE EXTENSION.

A more traditional Forms Feng Shui solution involves designing the Main Door to open in the direction of the flow of water (or traffic). This way, the house can still "catch" the Qi as it rides with the wind from one direction to the other. Again, examine the flow of traffic. If the house sits on a residential road, then this is not an issue. You only care if the house sits in front of a freeway or highway.

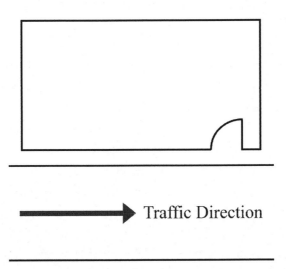

Traffic Direction

FIGURE 39: MAIN DOOR OPENS IN THE DIRECTION OF TRAFFIC.

These are common solutions, but they are only textbook examples and do not replace the value of an on-site assessment. There is so much more to it. And of course, merely locating mountain and water features provides the most elementary level, but it is a good starting point for your understanding of Forms Feng Shui.

NOTE FROM JEN: *The interactions of mountains (Yin) and waters (Yang) indicate the natural formation of Qi in the external environment. This is the core idea of Forms Feng Shui.*

BRIGHT HALL

The Bright Hall, also called "Ming Tang" in Chinese, is one of the most popular concepts in Feng Shui. Why? This is what facilitates the gathering of Qi before it enters the house through the Main Door.

By definition, the Bright Hall is an area with an open space directly in front of the house to allow Qi (harnessed from the external environment) to collect, gather, and settle. Just like water gathers in a pool, the open space must allow Qi to flow smoothly and ensure the transition occurs in a graceful and sentimental manner. This is the very idea of a Bright Hall.

As a rule, you generally want to see an open space that is free of obstruction.

FIGURE 40: A HOUSE WITH AN IDEAL BRIGHT HALL.

If a home or building is missing a Bright Hall, the lack of open space causes blockages and obstacles. This lack is common in compact urban cities where space is limited.

FIGURE 41: A PACKED METROPOLITAN CITY (NEW YORK CITY).

In ancient times, the solution to this scenario is to avoid living or working in a space that lacks a Bright Hall altogether. However, this is not always realistic in this overdeveloped and overcrowded world. As such, the most practical solution for this is to assess the Flying Star that influences the front side of the property to determine the severity of the situation. This will subsequently drive the most appropriate Feng Shui recommendation. More on Flying Star Feng Shui in Chapter 13.

MAIN DOOR

The Main Door of a property is another important stress point. Because the Bright Hall and the Main Door have a direct relationship, they play an active role influencing each other.

To start, the Main Door is considered the "Mouth of Qi." This is the initial entry point where life-sustaining energy (gathered from the Bright Hall) will enter and vitalize the space inside the home. Good external forms and Bright Hall must accompany a good Main Door in order to fully "tap into" positive Qi. One cannot be without the other.

Since the idea of the Main Door is to receive vital energy, naturally, the assessment would be to ensure there are no negative external structures (such as a tree or a pylon) blocking its way.

As a general rule, you want to evaluate the view directly from the Main Door looking out. To illustrate, stand in front of your Main Door facing out. Within your direct eye level (not peripheral), what do you see? Do you see a beautiful view? Is the space in front of you open, welcoming, and free of external obstructions? Or is your view obstructed with an oversized pillar, tree, lamppost, or some other unpleasant object?

When assessing the forms of the Main Door, we are evaluating the features within the boundaries of the Main Door. So when you are standing in front of the Main Door looking out, extend an imaginary line from the two sides of the Main Door directly outwards. If any negative forms are outside of these lines, then you do not need to be concerned with the effects of the features. Negative forms will only affect the strength of the Main Door if they are within those boundaries.

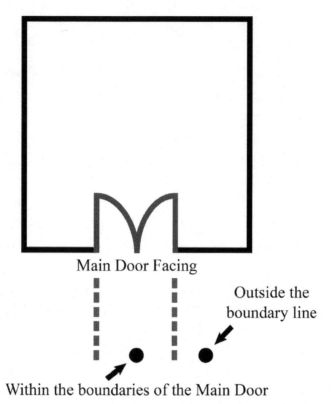

Main Door Facing

Outside the
boundary line

Within the boundaries of the Main Door

FIGURE 42: MAIN DOOR ILLUSTRATION SHOWING FEATURES
INSIDE AND OUTSIDE THE BOUNDARIES.

Scenario 1: "Piercing heart" obstruction: A Main Door that directly faces a tree, a lamppost, a pole, or a pillar is not considered favorable. It generates "Piercing Heart" Sha Qi. In simple terms, these features cause an otherwise sentimental (i.e., curved) Qi to "split" in half, piercing or cutting its way as it moves into the house. This adversely affects the career and wealth aspects of the residents.

FIGURE 43: MAIN DOOR FACING A TREE.

Solution: If the problem already exists in a home where you live, you have an option to remove the obstruction, relocate the Main Door to another section of the house, or install a screen door to redirect the Qi.

Scenario 2: Sharp corners and edges: You may encounter a Main Door that faces the sharp edges of a building or sharp corners of a building's roof. This sharp, pointy feature also creates Sha Qi or Poison Arrow, invariably affecting the quality of Qi.

FIGURE 44: MAIN DOOR FACING SHARP CORNERS AND EDGES.

Solution: Because a sharp corner or edge represents the Fire element, the cure would be to use the Earth element to help dissolve this feature. Some common Earth element objects include items shaped like a square, in earth-tone colors, or traditionally, by using the number 5 (because this number is also considered an Earth element), like installing five flagpoles.

NOTE FROM JEN: *Remember, the Productive Cycle of the Five Elements principles is the most preferred method in managing any Feng Shui issues. Without proper training, the Destructive Cycle could actually activate an unfavorable element, causing more harm and imbalances.*

Scenario 3: Narrow pathway: Some homes have a long, narrow pathway leading up to the Main Door. This pathway is not considered good because the narrow space "squeezes" the Qi from a free-flowing, circular movement into a sharp, piercing motion, encouraging the Qi to enter the house too quickly. This also creates Sha Qi or Poison Arrow.

FIGURE 45: PROPERTY WITH A LONG AND NARROW PATHWAY.

Solution: Because a long, straight pathway is classified as a Wood element in Feng Shui, the best way to address this challenge is by incorporating a Fire element, like a red color doormat or a red color door to weaken the strength of the Sha Qi. Otherwise, with the careful guidance of a professional, you can also use a round-shaped door at the entrance of the house. Because round objects are a Metal element, they will also control and destruct the negative Wood element energy produced from the narrow pathway.

It should be noted, however, that this type of Bright Hall is still considered less-than-ideal. As such, any cure or Feng Shui recommendations provided will help, but they won't be as strong and prosperous as having proper Bright Hall features.

Scenario 4: Shrubbery at main door: When the front area of the house is covered with messy foliage or blocked by heavy shrubs and trees, not only does this create dark shadows or lack of sunlight, but it prevents Qi from finding its way to the Main Door. Don't miss out on harnessing good Qi by preventing it from coming in!

Solution: If the home was already built with an open space, simply remove any overgrown plants or trees that might be blocking the façade of the house. Clear out the clutter near and around the Main Door, install bright lights, and create a happy and welcoming open space.

NOTE FROM JEN: *The recommendation to create open space in front of the Bright Hall should not give the impression that it should be completely bare and clear. The Red Phoenix (or Table Mountain) in front must be present in order to have some kind of Qi protection rather than an open space without any shelter.*

A Feng Shui consultant may encounter thousands of different challenges in his or her consultations. This is just a list of the ones most common with today's architectural designs. It is also important to note that the areas of the resident's life affected will depend on <u>where</u> the Main Door is located in relation to the Eight Trigrams, as well as the influences of the base and annual Flying Stars. A qualified Feng Shui practitioner will also know whether adding any other elementally enhancing features will be appropriate for the space.

NOTE FROM JEN: *Not every Feng Shui issue can be fixed; otherwise, you would never see a home with poor fortune. The bottom line is, the power of Feng Shui lies not always in "curing" or "fixing" things, but also in avoiding these negative features in the first place. Remember, Classical Feng Shui remedies have nothing to do with plopping down crystals and trinkets. The essence of benevolent Qi is derived first from the environment that also includes good external forms and positive Flying Stars.*

chapter 11

CLASSICAL FENG SHUI:
THE ESSENCE OF INTERNAL FORMS

"Allow yourself to see your home as an integral part of your existence rather than somewhere you simply return to at the end of each day." – UNKNOWN

Time to take your Feng Shui practice inside…

When I talk about the interior features of a property, I am not necessarily referring to the décor or design of furniture and other manmade gadgets inside the home. At least, not yet. Instead, I am drawing your attention first to the internal forms of the property's physical floor plan, infrastructure, as well as the locations and directions of key rooms.

While the rest of the house will obviously be analyzed as a whole, Classical Feng Shui places higher emphasis – or priority – on key areas. These are the Main Door facing in, kitchen, master bedroom, and any other rooms that are actively being used like a home office or meditation room.

Internal Forms assessment is an important step to help determine if the space allows for Qi to gather, settle down, and circulate around the whole house in a meander-like motion. A good practitioner will ensure benevolent Qi harnessed from outside is not wasted, trapped, leaked, or transformed into Sha Qi.

In this chapter, I want to highlight some common scenarios you may encounter in a conventional Feng Shui consultation as it relates to the internal forms of a property. And as an added bonus, I will confront a few popular myths that, unfortunately, continue to contribute to the confusion around the traditional Feng Shui practice.

MAIN DOOR (FACING IN)

Assessing the internal forms of the Main Door requires that you stand at the Main Door looking in. This way, you can focus on examining the features inside the home from this viewpoint. Ideally, you do not want to have any negative forms that may prevent, block, or repel positive Qi from entering.

Scenario 1: The Back Door or Back Window is directly visible from the Main Door: A direct alignment of the Main Door to the back door or back window should always be avoided. In that set-up, any Qi that comes in will immediately leave the house. This prevents positive Qi from nourishing and vitalizing the space inside.

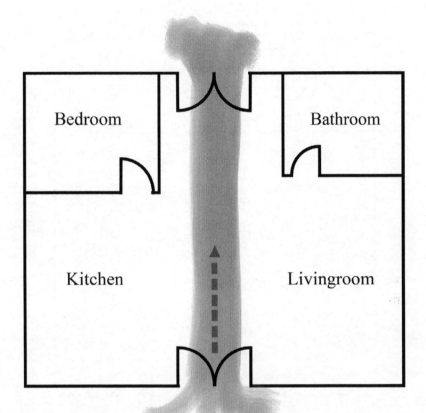

Main Door looking in

FIGURE 46: MAIN DOOR FACES BACK DOOR.

Solution: Create some kind of a blockage, such as a wall or an island, to redirect the Qi. Make it flow *around* the space, rather than directly out the back door or window.

Scenario 2: Back Windows are located in the back corner of the room: When back windows are located in a corner (creating a triangle-like form), the effect also permits Qi to quickly leak out of the backside of the house.

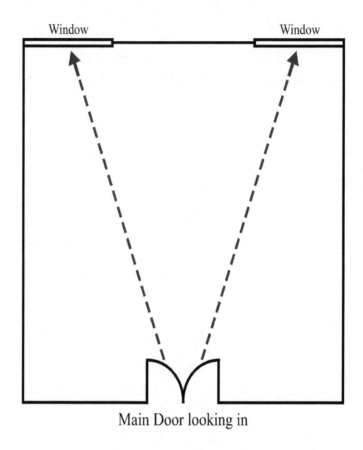

FIGURE 47: WINDOWS ARE PLACED IN THE BACK CORNERS.

Solution: Build a wall or place any type of large object – such as a cabinet or a fish tank –within the direct line to prevent Qi from escaping.

Scenario 3: The Main Door opens immediately to a room: When the Main Door opens directly into a room – whether it is a bathroom, a closet, a storage room, a home office, or a bedroom – Qi coming in essentially gets "trapped" there. This prevents it from circulating around the rest of the house.

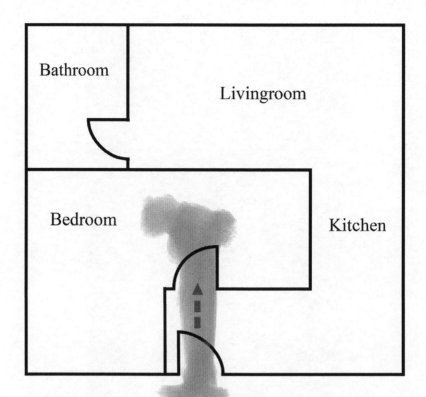

Main Door looking in

FIGURE 48: MAIN DOOR FACES A ROOM.

Solution: Ideally, you would not choose to have the Main Door face a room directly. And if you could influence the floor plan, you could prevent it. However, if this is unavoidable, the easiest and best solution is to keep the room's door closed whenever possible.

Scenario 4: The Main Door faces a staircase: When the Main Door opens up immediately to a staircase (either going up or down), Qi automatically flows upwards or downwards, overlooking the rest of the areas in the main house.

FIGURE 49: MAIN DOOR FACES A STAIRCASE.

Solution: Unless you can reposition or "open" a new Main Door (which is often unrealistic, especially for pre-constructed homes), this scenario generally does not have a traditional "Forms fix." In this case, the practitioner should assess the impact using Flying Star Feng Shui to determine the severity of this design challenge.

NOTE FROM JEN: *Keep the Main Door assessment simple. I have often encountered clients and even practitioners who overthink and overanalyze the smallest details that really have little or no negative impact. The idea behind the Main Door assessment is fairly straightforward. Just imagine how Qi will* *flow in and around the house upon entering the Main Door. Your goal is to keep this area open and free of negative obstructions that would trap, leak, block, or transform Qi into Poison Arrows.*

DEBUNKING THE MAIN DOOR MYTH

Myth: The famous Red Door: Many people in the West think you have to install a red door to have "good Feng Shui."

Myth Debunked: While the color red is auspicious in Chinese culture, elementally, the color also represents the Fire element. Whether or not you need a red-colored Main Door will depend on the time factor and direction of the property, among other things. Most sophisticated consultants will be able to determine formulaically whether Fire is a favorable element for the house. To put it bluntly, a red door is <u>not</u> always going to have a positive impact for every house, every time!

THE KITCHEN

The kitchen plays an important function in a house. This is where you prepare your food, gather with family, and nourish your body. Hence, when Qi is weak or negative, it has a direct impact on your health and overall happiness.

Many Feng Shui books tell you to assess the sink, island, microwave, and refrigerator, but these features do not represent the core function of the kitchen. Furthermore, this type of approach is unnecessary and overreaching. Just like the bed (where you sleep) is the key feature in a bedroom assessment, the stove (where you cook) is the highlight of the kitchen. Therefore, in the scenarios outlined below, we will be assessing the internal forms of the kitchen by the location of the stove.

That said, the Qi quality of the kitchen will depend on a number of possibilities, including the location and forms of the kitchen in relation to the entire property's floor plan, the external forms of the environment, and the formulaic calculations of the Flying Star Feng Shui. For now, let's skip over the details and focus on some general scenarios you may encounter.

Scenario 1: The kitchen stove is exposed: In the old days of house-building, the kitchen was treated like a treasure that needed to be kept hidden (like a safe where you keep your money and valuables). Therefore, the most ideal location for the kitchen is an area of the house that is not immediately exposed to the Main Door or too close to the main entrance of the house. If the kitchen is immediately visible, or has a direct alignment with the Main Door, this layout is not considered positive.

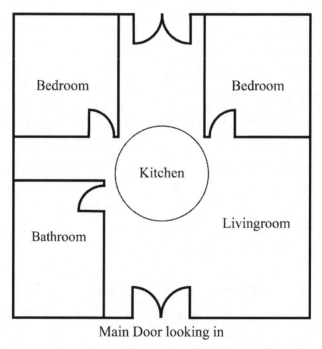

Main Door looking in

FIGURE 50: KITCHEN IS LOCATED IN THE CENTER OF THE HOUSE.

Solution: Create a blockage, such as a wall or other object placement, to prevent Qi from directly "hitting" the kitchen space. Or whenever possible, relocate the kitchen space to the backside of the house, rather than in the center.

Scenario 2: The kitchen stove faces out of the house: The kitchen stove is the source of energy. So the stove should face in – not out – to ensure Qi remains intact instead of leaking out.

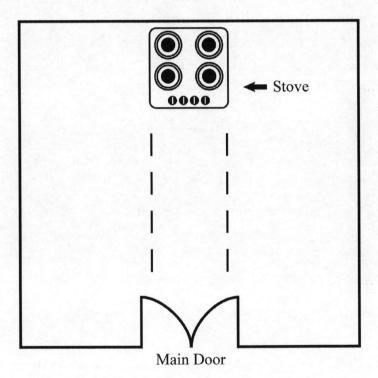

FIGURE 51: KITCHEN STOVE IS FACING OUT.

Solution: The easiest and simplest solution is to turn the stove or position it so that it faces into the house.

DEBUNKING THE KITCHEN MYTHS

Myth 1: The kitchen sink being directly across from the stove is bad: Many people think that when the sink (a Water element) is directly across from the stove (a Fire element), it will create a Water-Fire clashing relationship, thereby negatively impacting the people's health and overall wellbeing.

FIGURE 52: KITCHEN SINK AND STOVE ARE DIRECTLY ACROSS FROM EACH OTHER.

Myth 2: The kitchen sink being directly adjacent to the stove is bad: Similarly, when the sink (a Water element) and the stove (a Fire element) are positioned side-by-side, many also infer that the two kitchen features are in a conflicting, or conquering, relationship.

FIGURE 53: KITCHEN SINK AND STOVE ARE ADJACENT TO EACH OTHER.

You might ask: Why are they both myths?

Myth 1 and 2 Debunked: While Water and Fire do have a controlling relationship in accordance with the Five Elements theory, the relationship is not necessarily negative, especially in these scenarios. I offer a simple answer to both misconceptions. Because many Western consultants are unfamiliar with the advanced studies of Classical Feng Shui, they don't realize Water and Fire are actually <u>complementary</u>. Fire represents Yin, and Water represents Yang. In "The Book of Changes," the Water over Fire Hexagram is referred to as "Chi Chi." This formation represents that, after a state of confusion, the evolution of order and peace begins. In other words, they are actually harmonious. Therefore, the two scenarios described above do not have any impact on the Feng Shui of the kitchen, or the house, for that matter.

Myth 3: Knives should never be placed next to the stove: Similarly, many New Age consultants suggest that knives (a Metal element) have a clashing relationship if placed next to the stove (a Fire element).

Myth Debunked: Psychologically, knives are scary. They are sharp and can be dangerous weapons. When you think of it this way, they can certainly leave an unsettling feeling when many knives of all sizes are exposed in an open area. Other than that, knives have no Feng Shui effects related to Forms. So this is purely based on personal preference. Food for thought: Do all successful restaurants keep their knives hidden?

Myth 4: The kitchen should never be located in the northwest sector of the house: The northwest sector represents the Heaven trigram (or Metal element), according to the Later Heaven Ba Gua arrangement. So people think that a kitchen situated in this sector of the house suggests an aggressive conquering relationship (Fire melts Metal) that would negatively impact the health and happiness of its occupants.

Myth Debunked: This approach is not a universal solution, especially in Flying Star Feng Shui. Energy is a dynamic phenomenon that permeates, moves, and circulates as time passes. As a result, energy (good or bad) will not reside in one area of the house forever. Food for thought: Is it practical to say that every kitchen in every house on earth should never have a kitchen in the northwest sector?

THE MASTER BEDROOM

The bedroom is another important internal feature. It is a place of rest (Yin) where we replenish and restore our personal energy, so that we can be productive and healthy to pursue our life's endeavors (Yang).

Like the kitchen, it is important to have good external forms and have the room located in a suitable sector of the house. Remember, Classical Feng Shui is an outward-in assessment that starts from a bigger picture and moves inward. If we prioritize our assessment this way, positive external forms, for example, will negate the positioning of your bed.

Let's go over a few common bedroom layout challenges.

Scenario 1: The master bedroom is located at the front of the house: The front of the house, especially areas closest to the Main Door, will naturally have more Yang-like energy. Because rest is associated as Yin, it is not desirable to have a master bedroom located at the front of the house.

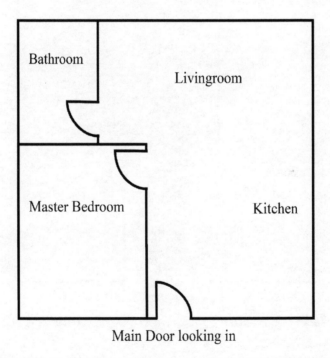

Main Door looking in

FIGURE 54: MASTER BEDROOM LOCATED AT THE FRONT OF THE HOUSE.

Solution: The most convenient solution is to switch bedrooms, if you have a secondary room. If this is not possible, then a consultant must employ the use of Flying Star calculations to assess the severity of the abstract energies in the space.

Scenario 2: The bed is directly in line with the bedroom doorway: When the bed is positioned directly in front of the bedroom doorway (either head-facing or feet-pointing), we are immediately impacted by the energy coming in without any barrier to slow down the Qi as we are trying to rest. This layout also creates Poison Arrow.

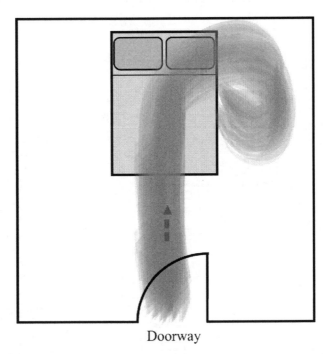

Doorway

FIGURE 55: THE BED IS DIRECTLY IN FRONT OF THE BEDROOM DOORWAY.

Solution: Reposition the bed away from the door or place an object, such as a folding screen, between the bed and the door.

Scenario 3: The bed is positioned at an angle against two walls: Some beds are positioned in an angle for aesthetics or when space is limited. This leaves your head directly exposed to (or "hit" by) Sha Qi when you're lying in bed, thereby disrupting sleep.

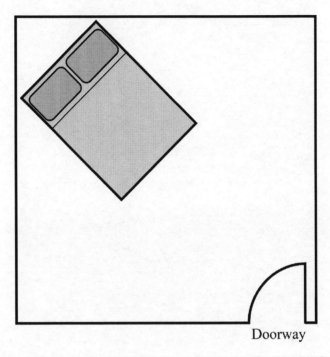

Doorway

FIGURE 56: THE BED IS POSITIONED AT AN ANGLE BETWEEN TWO WALLS.

Solution: Reposition the bed against a solid wall.

Scenario 4: The bed is underneath beams or another item: When beams (or other heavy objects) are directly above the bed, this will create a heavy or oppressed energy, affecting the quality of your rest.

FIGURE 57: THE BED IS POSITIONED DIRECTLY BELOW BEAMS.

Solution: Simply reposition the bed elsewhere in the room where it (and its occupants) is not impacted by the beams. If space is limited and you cannot move the bed, you can use a canopy to protect yourself from the heavy energy above. Also, as much as possible, avoid hanging anything directly above the bed, whether it's a ceiling fan, chandelier, or even wind chimes.

Scenario 5: The bed is directly below the windows: When the bed is positioned this way, it lacks support and protection.

FIGURE 58: THE BED IS POSITIONED DIRECTLY BELOW THE WINDOWS.

Solution: Reposition the bed so that the headboard side abuts a solid wall.

Scenario 6: The bed faces a mirror: Mirrors often has been associated with the Water element and "attract" energy; therefore, mirrors promote Yang-like energy in an otherwise Yin space.

FIGURE 59: THE BED IS POSITIONED DIRECTLY IN FRONT OF THE MIRROR.

Solution: Reposition the bed or remove the mirror so that it is not directly aligned in front of the bed.

DEBUNKING THE MASTER BEDROOM MYTHS

Myth 1: There should always be two bedside tables to promote love and romance: Many Black Hat Feng Shui practitioners will suggest that in order to invite the energy of romance and relationship in the bedroom, it is important to have two bedside tables rather than a single one, the latter symbolizing a "single" person.

Myth Debunked: Aesthetically, the room looks more balanced when there are two bedside tables. But otherwise, this thought process has nothing to do with internal forms. The deliberate action of placing a second nightstand does enhance the mindful intention of creating a special space for love and relationship, but this practice is more spiritual and psychological than it is scientific. Food for thought: If the dual bedside table theory was indeed true, does that mean all you have to do to fix any relationship trouble is to add an extra bedside table?

Myth 2: The direction of the headboard is the facing direction: Some teachings have suggested that the facing direction of the bed is where the head is situated within the bed.

Myth Debunked: When assessing the facing direction of the bed, the correct way is to follow where the feet are pointing. The logic behind this technique is that the headboard of the bed leans against a wall, providing solid support of mountain (similar to a house sitting against the Black Tortoise). On the other hand, where your feet are pointing represents the flow of water, such that once you sit up, the view in front of what you see is your facing direction (similar to a house facing toward the Red Phoenix).

chapter 12

CLASSICAL FENG SHUI: AN INTRODUCTION TO EIGHT MANSION

> *"Sometimes there are two very opposite directions, and we go with the stronger one at the end."* — MARC JACOBS

Eight Mansion (Ba Zhai or Pa Chai) is a fancy term that refers to a simple, widely used directional base system in Classical Feng Shui.

Under the theory of this practice, there are eight types of dwellings. Each type contains unique energy patterns that may be more suitable or beneficial to some people and not others. For this reason, the goal of Eight Mansion is to match the people (residents) to one of the "right" or most ideal property models (houses).

This technique involves a microanalysis of the internal property. It is used predominantly to assess the Qi of a property for its long-term effects (i.e., more than one year). It is particularly useful for property planning, like layout designs and renovations.

The Eight Mansion technique harnesses the knowledge of favorable and unfavorable compass directions and locations for each resident – ones they should "tap into" for good luck and ones they should avoid. Using your personal birth data, we can easily calculate your own personal favorable and unfavorable compass directions. This is called the *Life Gua Method*. Similarly, a house's favorable and unfavorable compass directions can also be calculated using the property's sitting direction (the *House Gua Method*). We will explore both methods and calculations later in this chapter.

Each person and house can therefore be assigned to two categories: East and West Groups.

Knowing which group you and your house "belong to" will help you determine: (i) whether the house you live in energetically supports you and (ii) which four directions are your "lucky" directions and which four are not. Then you can maximize your fortune by choosing to live in a house that best suits you, or tapping into your most favorable facing directions in most circumstances – or both.

In Eight Mansion, Forms continues to play an important role in how Qi influences the internal spaces. As such, the external environment factor cannot be neglected. Take, for example, two houses with the same facing directions. For illustration purposes, let's say both House A and House B face north. If the Main Door to House A faces a tree or a pillar that is creating some disruption in the flow of Qi collection, whereas House B does not have this feature, then it is easy to conclude that the Qi fortune to House A is weaker than House B, even though both face in the same direction.

One of the challenges of the Eight Mansion technique is that it does create a dilemma when one or more residents of the same household belong to two different groups (i.e., husband belongs to the East Group and wife belongs to the West Group). It can also cause problems if the person is residing in a house that belongs to a group different from his/her own (i.e., the house belongs to the East Group and the primary resident belongs to the West Group).

I've come across some folks, especially married couples or domestic partners, who panic when this is revealed. They're afraid they might have to sleep in separate bedrooms in the name of Qi! But the system is not meant to be applied in a "take it or leave it" fashion. Feng Shui, in any system, shouldn't force you to make silly or frivolous moves. A Feng Shui professional can assess these types of challenges and come up with a qualified solution tailored to the scenario.

One more note, and then we'll get to the good stuff, I promise. The technique I am about to describe is only a starting point to Eight Mansion Feng Shui. The system goes much deeper, with techniques like the Palace versus Star Method (Xing Gong Sheng Ke), along with the complicated component of time calculations (i.e., Flying Star Feng Shui). Nonetheless, this soft introduction will serve just fine for most enthusiasts looking to explore Feng Shui on their own.

So… how do you know what type of Qi to tap into for yourself?

EIGHT QUALITIES OF QI

Before you dive into the Gua (or Kua) calculations, you must understand there are eight types (or bodies) of Qi. These are also called *The Eight Wandering Stars*. The word "Star" in Feng Shui has a different meaning than its traditional definition. In Feng Shui, Stars are generally labeled with a number, a color, or an element, representing its own unique qualities. Let's walk through the high-level definition of each type of Qi by its Chinese and English translated name, as well as its traditional text name found in many Chinese books.

The Four Favorable Qi

Sheng Qi

English Name: Life Generating
Text Name: "Greedy Wolf"
Element: Wood

This is one of the most popular types of Qi, because it brings strong prosperous energy that attracts success, wealth, and prosperity luck. If you are looking to start a new project or business endeavor, gain money, want to make a change or get promoted in your career, or are making any other risky efforts that could use a little luck, it is meaningful to tap into this direction.

If it is work-related, it might be useful to place your work desk "facing" your personal Sheng Qi direction, or locate the Sheng Qi sector within your house and set up your home office there. For example, if your favorable Sheng Qi direction is north, you can position your work desk to face north, or locate a room in the north side of your house to set up your workstation, or both.

However, due to its dynamic Yang-like qualities, this is not the most beneficial Star to tap into for rest or sleep (Yin).

Tian Yi

English Name: Heavenly Doctor
Text Name: "Huge Door"
Element: Earth

Tian Yi is related to matters of health. Tap into this positive Star if you are looking to harmonize, bring balance, or improve your health and people relationships. You can do this by positioning your bed to face your Tian Yi favorable direction. Similarly, you can locate your Tian Yi favorable location within your house and have your bedroom there. For example, if your favorable Tian Yi direction is south, position your bed where your feet points south or design your master bedroom to sit in the south sector of your house.

This Star is also useful in attracting noblemen, such as mentors, teachers, and helpful people. It's an ideal one to tap into when you are looking to bring in all forms of help to further your career and wealth aspects.

Yan Nian

English Name: Longevity
Text Name: "Military Arts"
Element: Metal

The Yan Nian Star is useful when you want to establish good rapport, authority, or reputation in your job or community. It's also beneficial for improving personal relationships with friends and family and even romantic partners. Tap into this Qi quality to help build networking success and improve interpersonal communications with colleagues and customers, or if you're looking for love or wanting to improve current love matters. Again, position your bed and/or workstation accordingly.

Fu Wei

English Name: Stability
Text Name: "Assistant"
Element: Wood

Fu Wei symbolizes virtuous qualities, like calmness, tranquility, and serenity. It is a good one to harness if you are looking to feel more grounded and stable. The energetic quality is less active than its counterpart, Sheng Qi. Therefore, this is the ideal Star to tap into for activities "within the mind and body," like meditation and yoga, or if you are looking to feel more relaxed or cultivate more mental clarity. You can locate the Fu Wei sector of your house to set up a meditation room or for other Yin activities like reading or journaling.

The Four Unfavorable Qi

Huo Hai

English Name: Mishaps
Text Name: "Rewards"
Element: Earth

This Star is traditionally called "Rewards," but in truth, it is not an auspicious one. Huo Hai is responsible for harboring mishaps, negative and sudden changes, loss of wealth, and other obstacles and hindrances. It can create small annoyances, such as unexpected money outflow on house repairs, delays on projects, or people hassling you for no apparent reasons. It is best to avoid having your bedroom and office in this location and direction.

Wu Gui

English Name: Five Ghosts
Text Name: "Chastity"
Element: Fire

The naming irony continues with Wu Gui, or "Chastity." This Star is actually the culprit for bringing relationship troubles such as betrayal, backstabbing, malice, rumors and gossip, and intentional sabotage. This influence creates mistrust, disloyalty, miscommunication, and misunderstandings among people and family members in the same household. Avoid using this area of the house for important activities, like sleeping and cooking.

Liu Sha

English Name: Six Killings
Text Name: "Literary Arts"
Element: Water

Although the classic text name sounds positive, Liu Sha has nothing to do with academics or literary efforts. This negative Star is responsible for attracting misfortunes such as legal troubles, physical injuries and harms, medical surgeries, scandals, robberies, and other money problems. It is best to use this space for unimportant activities. Make it a storage room or garage.

Jue Ming

English Name: Life Threatening
Text Name: "Broken Soldier"
Element: Metal

This is perhaps the most negative or dangerous of the four unfavorable Qi. Jue Ming brings accidents, major illnesses and ailments, business failures, financial woes like bankruptcy and foreclosures, and serious relationship problems like divorce and breakups.

It is best to completely avoid purchasing a house where the Main Door faces this direction or is located in this sector.

NOTE FROM JEN: *These Stars are not always absolute. When more sophisticated applications of Eight Mansion are applied (including Forms), the interactions of these Stars will modify their original nature. Use my descriptions only as a starter's guide.*

THE RESIDENTS AND THE MEANING OF LIFE GUA

You can easily derive your personal Life Gua (or Ming Gua) mathematically from your birth information. Each Gua is unique to the individual, like your birthday, and will help determine your four favorable and four unfavorable compass facing directions.

Here's what goes into the calculation.

Lunar Calendar vs. Solar Calendar

One of the most common mistakes beginners make when calculating the Life Gua is using the Lunar Calendar rather than the Solar

Calendar. There is a great difference! The Solar Calendar focuses on the position of the Sun, while the Lunar Calendar is based on the moon. Because the Lunar Calendar does not run parallel with the Solar Calendar, every few years a thirteenth month is added to the Lunar to mathematically match the Solar. The Solar Calendar is always the point of reference for all Chinese Metaphysics practices (except for Purple Star Astrology).

Simply put, the Solar Calendar begins on a fixed date: the 4th of February of every year (also called the "Coming of Spring").

The confusion comes to bear for people born <u>before</u> February 4th. Let's say you were born on January 31st, 1980. Instead of using the year 1980, you must use the previous year, or 1979, as your starting point.

Calculating Life Gua

After you ascertain the birth year, factor in the sex of the person. Let's say you want to calculate the Life Gua of a male born in 1948. Here's how you can derive his Life Gua:

Add the first two digits of the birth year until you arrive at a single digit:
1 + 9 = 10 ... 1 + 0 = 1

Add the last two digits of the birth year until you arrive at a single digit:
4 + 8 = 12 ... 1 + 2 = 3

Add the two single numbers from the calculations above:
1 + 3 = 4

Then subtract it from 11 (constant) for male:
11 − 4 = 7

The resulting number is this man's Life Gua Number 7.

It's only slightly different for females: Instead of subtracting from 11, you add 4. Here is an example of a female born in 1980.

Add the first two digits of the birth year until you arrive at a single digit:
$1 + 9 = 10 \dots 1 + 0 = 1$

Add the last two digits of the birth year until you arrive at a single digit:
$8 + 0 = 8$

Add the two single numbers from the calculation above:
$1 + 8 = 9$

Then add 4 (constant) for female until you arrive at a single digit:
$4 + 9 = 13 \dots 1 + 3 = 4$

The resulting number is the woman's Life Gua Number 4.

If the resulting number is 5 – for either male or female – the Life Gua will automatically revert or assume the position of Life Gua Number 2 for male and Life Gua Number 8 for female. The reason? The Number 5 does not belong to any Gua or Trigram from the Luo Shu. In other words, the Number 5 does not have any direction.

East and West Group People
Once you have obtained the Life Gua Number, then you can assign the person as belonging either to the East or West Group.

Male or female, Life Gua Numbers 1, 3, 4, and 9 belong to the East. Numbers 2, 6, 7, and 8 belong to the West.

You may wonder why there is no North or South Group. The translation of these groups does not necessarily represent the literal meaning of the compass direction of East or West. These are just names used to demarcate the greater and lesser Yin and Yang transformation. In this case, East is considered Yang and West is Yin.

For the examples we calculated above, you can now see that the male with Life Gua 7 belongs to the West Group, and the female with Life Gua 4 belongs to the East Group.

After establishing the Life Guas, you can refer to the East and West Group reference tables at the end of this chapter to determine your four favorable and four unfavorable facing compass directions and assess whether the important sectors of your house (such as your Main Door, master bedroom, kitchen, and home office) are located ideally for you.

THE PROPERTY AND THE MEANING OF HOUSE GUA

Because this method is based on the house's orientation, start by determining the house's facing direction. This is an important first step – just like confirming the person's correct birth year according to the Solar Calendar for the Life Gua calculation.

You can get the house's facing direction with a simple compass. A traditional Luo Pan is not necessary for this, because you are not demarcating the direction using the 24 Mountains or other Feng Shui formulas.

Once you nail the correct facing direction, in which the house was meant to face, like the façade, the House Gua is exactly 180° the opposite direction. Simple as that. We call this the house's "sitting" direction.

To illustrate, let's say you're working with a house that your compass tells you faces north. The exact opposite direction is, of course, south. Now you can categorize the house as belonging either to the East or West Group, and see whether the house matches your personal Life Gua!

These houses belong to the East Group:

- House sitting north
- House sitting east
- House sitting southeast
- House sitting south

These houses belong to the West Group:

- House sitting southwest
- House sitting northwest
- House sitting west
- House sitting northeast

NOTE FROM JEN: *I like to say that Classical Feng Shui is not "instant noodles." With any body of knowledge, and especially science, one cannot deduce that the method provides a quick fix to life's messy challenges. Be mindful not to trade in quality for diluted "solutions."*

REFERENCE TABLES FOR LIFE GUA:
EAST AND WEST GROUPS

East Group Reference Table

Gua #	Sheng Qi	Tian Yi	Yan Nian	Fu Wei	Huo Hai	Wu Gui	Liu Sha	Jue Ming
1	SE	E	S	N	W	NE	NW	SW
3	S	N	SE	E	SW	NW	NE	W
4	N	S	E	SE	NW	SW	W	NE
9	E	SE	N	S	NE	W	SW	NW

West Group Reference Table

Gua #	Sheng Qi	Tian Yi	Yan Nian	Fu Wei	Huo Hai	Wu Gui	Liu Sha	Jue Ming
2	NE	W	NW	SW	E	SE	S	N
6	W	NE	SW	NW	SE	E	N	S
7	NW	SW	NE	W	N	S	SE	E
8	SW	NW	W	NE	S	N	E	SE

chapter 13

CLASSICAL FENG SHUI:
AN INTRODUCTION TO FLYING STAR

> *"Our life experiences show there are ups and downs in fortune. No house can have good fortune forever. This is because our wellbeing is not only affected by the physical shapes in our environment, but we are also under the influence of certain abstract energies which we cannot see, but they exist everywhere in the environment."* – GRAND MASTER RAYMOND LO

I have been revisiting the importance of examining the influence of both the landscape (Forms) and time and space (Compass). We're building to something here. Ultimately, the power of Feng Shui lies in the <u>combination</u> of both the physical surroundings and the abstract energies – the forces of things we cannot see.

It helps explain the <u>timing</u> of the elements, which is something I often see missing from simpler Feng Shui styles used in the West.

Mastering this technique is important because, in effect, understanding how Qi moves inside a property helps us pinpoint the strengths, weaknesses, and even the potential of any property. Thus, it empowers us to better predict upcoming events, including revealing hidden information that may affect the health, wealth, and relationship aspects of those who occupy the space.

In this chapter, we will tie in several concepts I have covered throughout the book (including the Luo Shu, Ho Tu, Five Elements, Yin and Yang, the Eight Trigrams, Later Heaven Ba Gua, time factor and Solar Calendar, property facing direction, and the Luo Pan). Yes, it's a lot to consider! But you will finally see how the pieces come together that form the core foundation of the Flying Star Feng Shui system.

NOTE FROM JEN: *Flying Star is one of the most widely practiced systems used by Classical Feng Shui practitioners today.*

INTUITION VS. LOGICAL DEDUCTION

In the West, many New Age practitioners use personal intuition to assess the Feng Shui of a space. You might hear one say, "This room *feels* really great." Or "This area just *feels* off."

Although there is an advantage to tapping into your human instincts for Feng Shui, this approach offers nothing in the way of an objective or systematic explanation as to *why* the good or bad fortune is flowing. Besides, one person's experience (or feelings) will differ significantly from another's. As such, this method, I find, offers discrepancies and inconsistencies. It further contributes to the confusion on what Feng Shui is truly all about and leads people to lump it in as a form of divination (a superstition or religion).

That's why I like Flying Star Feng Shui so much.

NOTE FROM JEN: *Feng Shui Master and author Stephen Skinner once explained, "Divination is an attempt at determining <u>what</u> is in store for you; Feng Shui is an active practice to find out <u>why</u> you have the luck you have – and to change it."*

Flying Star removes the "randomness" that arises when you're dealing with strictly abstract concepts. It's scientific. It uses logical deduction to assess how good and bad luck are distributed over time, such as why the fortune of a house changes from one year or one period to the next. It also helps pinpoint the causes of variations – or fluctuations, if you will – in your human experience in the same house over time.

Personally, I do embrace the intuitive side as I practice Feng Shui. Tapping into this side of my personal human experience allows me to truly become one with my environment. However, I also deeply crave the *science* behind the *feelings*. Why do some spaces feel good? Is it the ambience of the colors and plush fabric of the furniture that uplift my spirit? And why do I avoid certain spaces that give out spooky or creepy feelings? Is it the dark hallway, dim lighting, or uncomfortable décor?

Still, this kind of questioning is limited. It applies to only one aspect – the physical objects in my surroundings. It is one-dimensional. As a practitioner, I have encountered many new, beautiful homes with expensive, spa-like, and colorful décor that suffer from misfortune. I have also seen simple, older, and modest homes that are flowing with good luck.

It begs the question: Is interior decorating and placement of objects <u>based on feelings</u> enough to conclude on the Feng Shui of a house?

The answer is, definitely no.

I recognize that the interior design of a home does have a psychological impact. That should not be ignored. But it's not the whole story. Flying Star Feng Shui helps determine the invisible life force that is moving and flowing inside a home because it assumes there is a very real link between the present time, the time the home was built, the property's directional orientation (in terms of *where* the Qi is coming from), the changing luck of its residents, and yes, the physical objects inside the home.

That's why, as I deepened my own understanding of the philosophy, it became very important – even critical – to understand the abstract forces through a systematic approach, not just in a "touchy feely" way. I find that using both methods – intuition and science – offers the most concrete, substantial, and powerful evaluation when helping people and their spaces.

THE PRINCIPLES OF FLYING STAR FENG SHUI

Like its counterpart, Eight Mansion, Flying Star Feng Shui ensures that residents' important activities (such as sleeping, eating, and studying) are done in rooms or parts of the property with favorable (or positive) Stars.

Because Flying Star is concerned with the Qi quality over time and how Qi comes from different directions (embodying different qualities of Qi), the technique boils down to two important components: Time and Space. Time is calculated using the Chinese Solar Calendar, and direction is measured with a Luo Pan compass.

Time is constantly changing and moving. Therefore, the Flying Star technique is much more dynamic where changes can manifest almost immediately. Despite its ever-changing nature, time does move in a cyclical pattern (as I demonstrated in Chapter 9 with the explanation of Three Periods and Nine Ages). Because of this pattern, we can accurately predict or forecast how the changes will affect the Feng Shui of our environment at any given time. This is one advantage that is especially useful in allowing us to plan and adjust our surroundings to "flow" with the energy.

To understand how Qi moves within a space, there are two important pieces of information you must have before you can draw a Flying Star chart for a property: 1) the age and 2) the facing direction. Let's take a closer look.

Age of Property
The concept of Age of Property has many differing and even contradicting definitions.

The Flying Star chart is like the natal chart of a person being born. A house also has a "birth date" when it was constructed. The age of the property therefore helps form the base of the Flying Star Chart. (Stay with me on this subject, we will circle right back.)

One popular myth circulating the Classical Feng Shui world is that you can change the age of the property. Can a person change his or her birthday? Superficially, maybe, with makeovers and medicine. Realistically, no. A birth date never changes. The same applies to your house, regardless if it was improved, renovated, or had additions put on. The Age of Property never changes.

Food for thought: If you had plastic surgery done to your face, does that mean you also have a new birth date? If a person was born without limbs and subsequently had artificial limbs surgically added, is that person now younger?

That's a silly notion, but I offer such a dramatic illustration because this misconception endures in the industry today. There's an ongoing and heated debate over the age of property. Although the root source of such debate is unclear, it does raise a few eyebrows by those who honor the authentic approach. So here's the bottom line.

The age of a property can only be changed when the house is completely demolished and rebuilt. To suggest anything otherwise is cheating. If you could simply change the age of a property (like the destiny in your birthday) as easily as upgrading or renovating, then couldn't every single house in the world always be in good fortune? That idea does not seem logical.

In any case, determining the correct age of the property is crucial. It is one of two factors that establish the base energy that stays with that property forever (or until the house is demolished). When a house is constructed (like when a fetus is conceived), it essentially captures the energy of that period in time.

If you refer back to the concept of Three Periods, Nine Ages in Chapter 9, you'll recall that each 20-year stretch falls under one particular Age. Here's that table again.

A Cycle (180 Years)		
Upper Period	**Middle Period**	**Lower Period**
Age 1 (1864 – 1883)	Age 4 (1924 – 1943)	Age 7 (1984 – 2003)
Age 2 (1884 – 1903)	Age 5 (1944 – 1963)	Age 8 (2004 – 2023)
Age 3 (1904 – 1923)	Age 6 (1964 – 1983)	Age 9 (2024 – 2043)

So if a house was built in 2014, the age of the property is 8. If you moved into a house that was built in 1980, then the age of the property is 6, and so forth.

One more important point about the property's age. The crux of this "age" concept lies not only in the date the house was constructed, but also when the house was <u>first occupied</u>. For instance, if a house was built in 1983 (Age of 6) but was left unoccupied until the first residents moved in in 1984, then the correct age of property is Age of 7, not Age of 6.

So why is this? Different schools and teachers offer different explanations. However, I professionally associate it with Qi first getting "stimulated" when the people moved in (similar to when a person arrives at his or her first Luck Pillar in a Destiny Analysis).

This is very important to decipher because the base number in the Flying Star chart, which is the Age of Property, will dictate how Qi moves in the home. Getting this wrong is like setting up an incorrect formulaic template. It will calculate and produce incorrect results throughout, thereby affecting the accuracy of the Feng Shui assessment and subsequent recommendations.

Facing Direction of a Property
In Chapter 9, I explained the importance of establishing the property's facing direction (which is not always the Main Door of the house). When you have determined the true facing of the property, you will use a traditional Feng Shui Compass to take the measurements.

Sorting out whether the house's facing direction is north, east, south, or west is not enough in Flying Star Feng Shui. Only a traditional Luo Pan can demarcate a measurement that's meaningful by further dissecting the cardinal directions into sub-sectors, such as N1, N2, N3, etc.

By the way, you have to measure the facing direction of the entire property, regardless of if you are doing the Feng Shui of a single-story family house, a unit in a high-rise condominium, or a single office space in a commercial building. Focus on the full building.

THE NINE STARS

Before we dive into drawing the Flying Star chart, I want to share one more fascinating piece about the Stars in Flying Stars. To start, the word "Stars" is often used in Classical Feng Shui to refer to the type or body of Qi and is often symbolized numerically (e.g., 1 to 9) or by its Star name (e.g., Covetous Wolf, Military Career, etc.).

The Nine Stars essentially represent the energies we feel on earth that reflect the seven real astronomical stars of the Big Dipper (or Northern Ladle). It is a part of the Great Bear (Ursa Major) constellation that includes two other invisible stars, also known as the two "Assistant Stars."

The Big Dipper is an important force in Classical Feng Shui because in the ancient days, it was seen as a giant universal clock in the heavens. It regulated the waxing and waning of the seasons, Yin and Yang, and the Five Elements.

These clusters of stars appear to point to and circulate around the Pole Star, also known as the Polaris. This star has a fixed point, very close to the North Celestial Pole (or the center of the stars), hence, the Chinese marked this as the center of the sky – or center of the universe – because it can be seen from anywhere, at any location, on earth.

FIGURE 60: THE NINE STARS OF THE BIG DIPPER.

THE MEANING OF THE STARS

In Chapter 8, I included a table of the Eight Trigrams that correlated with a single number from 1 to 9. I will expand on that table here as you begin to dive deeper into Flying Star Feng Shui.

No.	Element	Person	Object	Body	Effects
1	Water	Middle-aged Man	Den, Blood	Ear, Kidney	Academic, Distant Luck
2	Earth	Elder Woman	Earth, Ox	Stomach	Sickness
3	Wood	Eldest Son	Thunder	Foot, Hair, Liver	Anger
4	Wood	Eldest Daughter	Wind, Rope	Buttocks, Neck	Romance
5	Earth	-	Sh'a	-	Misfortune
6	Metal	Elder Man	Heaven	Head, Lungs	Legal
7	Metal	Young Girl	Lake	Mouth	Scandal
8	Earth	Young Boy	Mountain	Hands	Current Luck
9	Fire	Middle-aged Woman	Beauty	Eyes, Heart	Coming Luck

HOW TO DRAW A FLYING STAR CHART

Similar to the Luo Shu diagram set up, the Flying Star Chart has nine equally divided squares. Each square (or Palace) represents a Trigram, a direction, a number, as well as the definition of the particular abstract energy that is residing in and influencing that area.

Once you have determined the two pieces of information about the property you're assessing (Age and Facing Direction), then you can draw its Flying Star chart.

Let's look at an example: A property was built in 1980 and has a north (N2) facing direction.

Step 1:
Draw a nine-square grid and place the directions in their appropriate spots, with south on the top, north at the bottom, east on the left, and west to the right.

Step 2:
Insert the Age of Property in the center. Based on the Three Periods, Nine Ages table, year 1980 is Age of 6. Therefore, the number 6 goes in the center Palace.

Step 3:
Fill in the rest of the grid by following the Luo Shu Path. You can also refer to Figure 19 in Chapter 8.

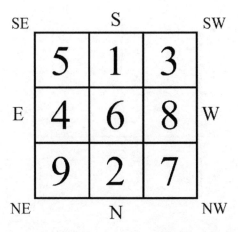

FIGURE 61: FLYING STAR CHART WITH STAR 6 IN THE CENTER.

Step 4:

The next step is a bit more involved. We must take into consideration the facing <u>and</u> sitting directions of the property.

This house has a N2 (or north sub-sector 2) facing direction; therefore, its sitting direction is exactly 180° from that, or S2 (south sub-sector 2).

In this example, the building is north facing with Star 2 residing in that Palace. Place the facing number in the center Palace on the right-hand side because this is the facing number of the house (Yang). It now takes the position of a Water Star, or Water Star 2 (WS2).

Similarly, you will take Star 1 residing in the south side, and place the sitting number in the center Palace on the left-hand side because this is the sitting number of the house. It now takes the position of a Mountain Star, or Mountain Star 1 (MS1).

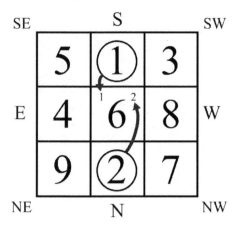

FIGURE 62: FLYING STAR CHART WITH WATER AND
MOUNTAIN STARS IN THE CENTER.

NOTE FROM JEN: *The facing direction of a property is considered active (Yang), and the sitting direction is considered inactive (Yin). In a Flying Star chart, a number that sits on the right-hand side is called "Water Star" and represents active energy (or Yang). On the other hand, a star that sits on the left-hand side is called "Mountain Star" and represents passive energy (or Yin).*

Step 5:

There is one more technique to master in order to complete the chart, and that is to determine which direction the stars will "fly" (ascending or descending).

Number	Sector 1	Sector 2	Sector 3
Odd (Yang)	Ascend (+)	Descend (-)	Descend (-)
Even (Yin)	Descend (-)	Ascend (+)	Ascend (+)

From Step 4 above, you will "fly" WS2 in ascending order because it is an even number (Star 2) and the house faces sector 2 (N2).

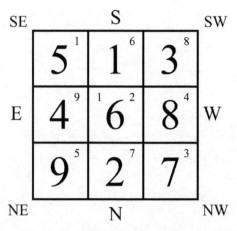

FIGURE 63: FLYING STAR CHART WITH WATER STARS.

Similarly, MS1 will fly in descending order because it is an odd number (Star 1) and the house belongs in sector 2 (S2).

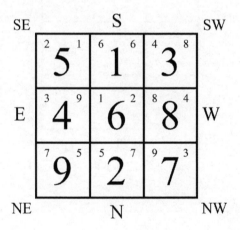

FIGURE 64: COMPLETE FLYING STAR CHART FOR AN AGE OF 6 PROPERTY.

NOTE FROM JEN: *There is one important exception to this rule. When Star 5 is in the center, you cannot assume 5 is an odd number. Because 5 does* *not belong to any Trigram, you have to observe what "gender" the Age is. If a house is Age 3 (odd), it will assume an odd number, and you fly the stars in that order. Conversely, if a house is Age 6 (even), then it will assume an even number.*

Congratulations! You have now formed the base Flying Star chart for our sample property.

Let's try another example: Age of 2, NE1 facing direction.

Here is the base chart with 2 in the center Palace.

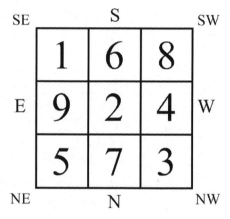

FIGURE 65: FLYING STAR CHART WITH STAR 2 IN THE CENTER.

Here is the complete chart with NE1 facing and SW1 sitting directions. Note that number 5 takes the Water Star position in the center Palace. Since the age of the property is an even number, you will fly WS5 as it assumes an even number position.

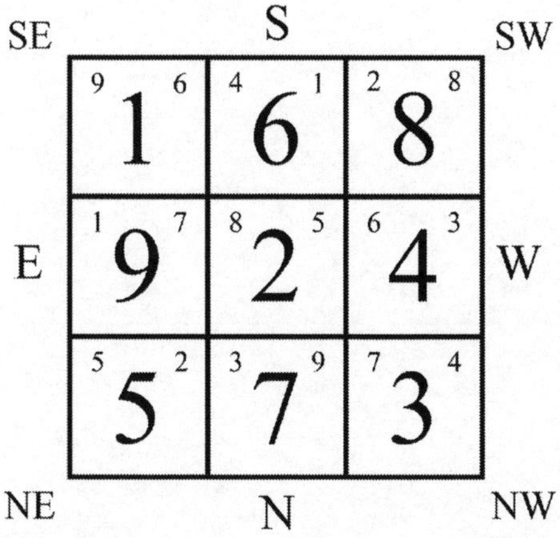

FIGURE 66: COMPLETE FLYING STAR CHART FOR AN AGE OF 2 PROPERTY.

This takes practice. And while practice does make perfect, as you can see from the illustrations above, you must first get the age and facing direction right to correctly compute the chart and do the corresponding analysis.

NOTE FROM JEN: *I have deliberately excluded discussions on interpreting and evaluating the Flying Stars to remain true to the introductory nature of this book. If you intend to explore this practice deeper, I highly recommend Grand Master Raymond Lo's book, "Feng Shui Essentials." It is written specifically for serious students and practitioners with a deeper discussion on Flying Star Feng Shui.*

chapter 14

CONTEMPORARY FENG SHUI: BLACK HAT

> *"Address the energy needs of the heart of your home, and you will find your home as a whole is soon imbued with a new harmoniousness that manifests itself indelibly in your existence."* — MADISYN TAYLOR

Nowadays, people use the term "Feng Shui" so loosely, especially in the West, that it has lost its traditional meaning. Phrases like "Fashion Feng Shui" – showing you how to apply the art to your personal wardrobe! – or "Feng Shui Your Wallet" further add to the long list of confusion.

But the biggest perpetrator of all is Black Hat Feng Shui.

Black Hat Feng Shui (BTB or Black Hat) was conceived by the late Grand Master Lin Yun and developed in the '70s. While this Feng Shui style is not found anywhere in Asia, its popularity grew in the '90s when the West began to embrace the idea of Feng Shui, however diluted.

Black Hat is an internal analysis application; as such, the system does not account for the external Forms of the environment that you would find in a Classical Feng Shui assessment. Black Hat disregards the direction and location of the property's facing direction, Main Door, as well as the most fundamental concept of Qi and the factor of time.

Because it does not observe the traditional cardinal directions of the environment and property, this system does not make use of a Luo Pan. Instead, the Eight Aspirations Map was developed as an essential tool used in Black Hat (similar to the idea of using the Luo Pan in Classical Feng Shui). Black Hat only concerns itself of the orientation or entry point of the door in any rooms every time for every property, regardless of which direction it faces or where it is located.

Many traditionalists question this method, because it deviates significantly from the core principles of the practice. They regard Black Hat as a "do-it-yourself" Feng Shui.

The point of this chapter is to outline the primary differences. That way, if you are interested in incorporating Feng Shui in your life as a hobbyist or enthusiast, or even developing a career, you can detect and tell the difference between the authentic and "new age" practice.

ALL ABOUT THE EIGHT ASPIRATIONS MAP

The Eight Aspirations Map gets confused with the traditional "Ba Gua" used in Classical Feng Shui. The main reason for the confusion comes from the name itself. The word *Ba Gua* literally translates to "eight trigrams." While the original concepts used in the Eight Aspirations Map are indeed "borrowed" from the classic Ba Gua Map, they are not identical and do not have a direct correlation to the ancient text of the Early or Later Heaven Ba Guas (as described in Chapter 8).

The Black Hat system believes that people have eight fundamental needs, or aspirations, in life. Therefore, the Eight Aspirations Map is regarded as a kind of "energy map," useful in mapping out life's eight most essential blessings and where they are located inside your home. This way, when different parts of your life demand attention, you can conveniently pinpoint the spaces that represent that aspect of your life and concentrate on enhancing the Qi in that space. So if you begin to hear things like how to look for the "love corner" or "wealth corner" in your house, then you can immediately recognize that this is a Black Hat practice, not Classical Feng Shui.

Let's talk about what each Aspiration means and how it corresponds to the different aspects of life.

Wealth & Prosperity	Fame & Reputation	Love & Marriage
Rear Left Blues, Purples, Reds	Rear Middle Reds	Rear Right Reds, Pinks, White
Health & Family	**Center Earth**	**Creativity & Children**
Middle Left Blues & Greens	Yellow & Earthtones	Middle Right White & Pastels
Knowledge & Self-Cultivation	**Career**	**Helpful People & Travel**
Front Left Black, Blues, Greens	Front Middle Black & Darktones	Front Right White, Grays, Black

↑ Entrance Quadrant ↑

FIGURE 67: THE EIGHT ASPIRATIONS MAP.

Health and Family

Health and Family (H&F) focuses on enhancing the quality of your relationship with your family and improving the vitality of your health and theirs. This definition includes your relationship with immediate and extended family – people like your siblings, aunts and uncles, grandparents, and cousins. The element associated with this Aspiration is Wood.

Wealth and Prosperity

Wealth and Prosperity (W&P) focuses on your ability to generate and retain money. While it does literally translate to wealth of money, it can also promote wealth and abundance in business opportunities, relationships, and other blessings.

Fame and Reputation

Fame and Reputation (F&R) focuses on your success and ability to achieve recognition in the workplace and in the community. This is especially useful when you are looking to get a promotion or become known for your work in your community. The element associated with this Aspiration is Fire.

Love and Relationship

Love and Relationship (L&R) focuses on your intimate relationships with your spouse or significant other. It can also be used to enhance or promote loving energy for friendships and for yourself.

Creativity and Children

Although Creativity and Children (C&C) has a direct correlation to bearing children, it is also an appropriate one to nurture the "birth" of new ideas, so it is great if you are looking to take on a new venture or business or nurture creativity. The element associated with this Aspiration is Metal.

Helpful People and Travel

Helpful People and Travel (HP&T) focuses on the concept of synchronicity: meeting the right people at the right time. This space enhances the energy for you to connect with and meet people who will inspire, mentor, and promote you. You can also focus on cultivating good luck for opportunities to travel for leisure, work, or relocating to a new area.

Career

Career (C) has a direct association with your professional endeavors to generate income for the home and to support the family. The element associated with this Aspiration is Water.

Knowledge and Self-Cultivation

Knowledge and Self-Cultivation (K&SC) focuses on cultivating a deeper sense of self, spiritually or religiously. It is beneficial if you are soul-searching or looking for a new direction in life.

Center (Earth)

The center represents the core of your being. It is the balance that holds everything together. This is an important one to focus on if you are looking to feel more grounded, secure, and stable in any aspect of your life. Naturally, the element associated with this Aspiration is Earth.

HOW TO USE THE EIGHT ASPIRATIONS MAP

To use the Map, you will perform three simple steps.

First, get a birds-eye view of your house to determine the overall shape of the property. Most houses will be shaped like a square or rectangle. However, there are some that have complex or obscure shapes, like a T, L, S, or U, or other shapes with protruding sections of the house. The goal is to create a perfect square-like shape that hovers over the entire floor plan. Therefore, it is important to outlay the Map so that every part of the house is inside the square.

Second, stand in front of the entrance and face the house – as if you are about to step inside. Because the primary entrance is considered the "mouth of Qi," a vital entry point for Qi, this is how you want to orient the Map for the whole structure. This is still true even if you normally enter from the backyard, side door, or garage. In contrast to Classical Feng Shui, the Map does not follow the facing façade of the building; rather, you always follow the direction of the Main Door.

Third, divide the floor plan into nine equal squares, like a tic-tac-toe board, locating the eight blessings (and the center) in your home. Once you have the basics down, it is fairly simple to map any structures from this point on.

LET'S CLEAR THE AIR ABOUT BTB

Black Hat has become the source of most, if not all, of the misunderstandings around the traditional practice of Feng Shui. In this section, I want to discuss some of the more popular myths and misconceptions it's given rise to. I hope this will become a turning point in your ability to ferret out the deviations from the authentic practice.

The "Feng Shui" application of the Black Hat system, for one, focuses on associating the internal structure and design of your home with the eight aspects of life by observing the objects, décor, and arrangements of furniture inside the home. For this reason, the authentic practice of Feng Shui often gets confused with being an interior decorating assessment. That's unfortunate and even offensive. Most Feng Shui practitioners are not trained interior designers.

Here's one I hear all the time from laypeople: "If you want to incorporate Feng Shui in your life, then it is imperative to install a red door on your house." Hardly! While the color red is considered auspicious in Chinese culture, elementally, the color red is also representative of the Fire element. But, as you already know from reading this book, a red door is not necessarily positive for all homes. Depending on the time factor and direction of the property, for instance, the Fire element at the front of the house may actually be harmful.

A house may need a Water element to boost the Qi at the Main Door; as such, the recommendation may be to install a water feature such as a fountain. Or, if the house is encountering negative Earth element, then the recommendation may be to introduce the Five Elements "Weakening Cycle" by installing a metal wind chime to dissolve the negative Earth Qi at the front of the house (Metal exhausts Earth).

The aesthetics of your home, while they do have an impact on human psychology, are not a complete system. At least, not in Classical Feng Shui. The aesthetics are subjective. They depend on individual tastes and preferences, rather than an objective, systematic application of core Feng Shui principles.

Moreover, because Black Hat focuses on observing the objects surrounding a space, it also makes use of crystals, wind dancers, sound makers, and other gadgets. Unfortunately, these trinkets have also been confused with being a traditional Feng Shui "cure."

The use of crystals and the like is all part of the "new age" development in the West. It has no direct association with the Eastern auspicious commodities, which (although this is a surprise to most people) are traditionally more inconspicuous and hidden in nature.

The true power of the authentic practice is in its subtlety.

The idea is not to draw attention to the fact that a home has been "Feng Shui'd." The goal is to create a home that is comfortable and pleasing to the residents. At any rate, not everyone resonates with hanging crystals and dragon features within view!

I think the best description of this is in Grand Master Raymond Lo's book *Feng Shui Essentials*. He articulated explained, "The best Feng Shui design should not be easily detectable. It should give people an impression of ordinary comfort without [being] consciously aware of any conspicuous Feng Shui tricks or objects purely for Feng Shui purposes. If one enters a house and his immediate impression is that the household has employed Feng Shui, [then] there must be something odd or extraordinary in the design, and such design defeats the ultimate goal of Feng Shui, which is to create a comfortable and harmonious environment."

As you're probably gathering by now, Black Hat is more a spiritual practice than a scientific one. For instance, in order to properly use the Eight Aspirations Map, the system requires that you incorporate your "inner self" while designing the "Feng Shui" of the house. You will often be asked to "go within" or to do some soul-searching to align your authentic self and personal intentions with your home, and then use physical objects to help manifest them. This is just fine. And most of us do this, anyway. But let's not call it Feng Shui!

Not surprisingly, the application of this notion creates vast inconsistencies in the practice. That's because every individual is unique. How you design your space, aesthetically or intuitively, is up to you – and you alone. If you are assessing the Feng Shui of a single man's residence, for instance, and he is looking to enhance his love life matters, it might seem a bit silly to suggest he decorates the Love and Marriage sector of his house with pink-colored objects and a pair of doves, or to hang pictures or arts of loving couples. Similarly, some women are not receptive to pink objects either. And this is just one aspect that makes this style more difficult to apply to the masses.

You already know that the traditional practice of Feng Shui follows a series of steps and calculations that, when tempered with a hint of intuition, can make real, tangible improvements in people's lives. Above all, the application of the core principles is scientific and the same every time. That's exactly why I love Feng Shui. And I hope you will too.

chapter 15

CONTEMPORARY FENG SHUI: SPACE CLEARING

> *"Our homes are mirrors of ourselves. Through them we can interface with the universe."* — DENISE LINN

Space Clearing is a practice you'll hear about as you study Feng Shui. It's intended to protect the residents from misfortunes or spiritual afflictions. Traditionally called "House Blessings," it emphasizes harmonizing the flow of energy in spaces on a much deeper or spiritual level. Space Clearing has its roots in Shamanism and ancient spiritual and religious practices in many old cultures in Bali, India, Peru, and Morocco.

What Space Clearing is not – though many in the West don't realize this – is a sub-system or part of "the art of Feng Shui." In fact, Space Clearing has nothing to do with Feng Shui at all.

Space Clearing became popular in the West when Feng Shui was commercialized. While the source of the idea that Space Clearing needed to be integrated in the practice of contemporary Feng Shui is unknown, many New Age practitioners, like Karen Kingston in the U.K. or Karen Rauch Carter in the U.S., for example, advocate incorporating Space Clearing techniques. And it is common to find New Age Feng Shui practitioners who are also certified Space Clearing experts.

Space Clearing takes many forms. One example is found in the Christian faith, when an ordained priest will come to the house to bless it with holy water and prayers. In Hinduism, a Hindu priest incorporates chants and mantras, boiling of cow's milk, and prayers to Lord Ganesha (the elephant-headed deity who removes obstacles and ensures success in the endeavors of humans). These blessings symbolize a new beginning for the new residents and for initiating positive energy and good fortune.

In the West, you may encounter "space healers." They employ various techniques, such as smudging, flower offerings, burning incense, clapping, bell or gong ringing, salt burning, and even aromatherapy. These acts are supposed to clear the energy paths within a space. But again, Space Clearing is entirely different and separate from the philosophy of Feng Shui.

So why is there a whole chapter devoted to it here?

The relationship is sometimes described like this: If you do Feng Shui without Space Clearing, it's like putting a fresh bouquet of flowers in a vase filled with dirty water. Before employing the works of Feng Shui (the flowers), it is often recommended that the space be cleared of the old or residual energy (dirty water) of the previous residents, or in some cases, any trauma that happened in the house, like sickness, death, violence, or spiritual disturbances.

One popular application is clearing the energy of your furniture and belongings, antiques, and hand-me-downs. The reasoning here is that the objects you keep are attached to the abstract energies imprinted by the current and previous owners, such as their human emotions, and the environmental circumstances surrounding these objects.

Another trendy idea in the West is Clutter Clearing. It has a similar connotation to Space Clearing, except it focuses on the physical level, rather than the abstract. Dust, dirt, unorganized items around the house, messy closet spaces, and garages are examples of things and spaces that need to be "decluttered."

Clutter can be mild. It can also reach massive proportions. Some people with compulsions are unable or unwilling to let go of (throw away) large quantities of items they don't need – even at the expense of their health, safety, and relationships. If you've seen the popular American television show "Hoarders" on A&E, you know just how out of control it can get. Energetically speaking, that clutter is said to create "stuck" or stale energy that drains your energy and hinders your ability to move forward in life.

You may come across articles and advertisements that call Clutter Clearing a subset of Feng Shui. However, again, there is no direct connection that links it with Feng Shui in the ancient texts.

While both Space Clearing and Feng Shui do touch on "energy" work, they are not the same. And my point is, let's give each practice their individual credit! Remember, Classical Feng Shui originated from China as a systematic "body of knowledge" used to evaluate Yin and Yang Houses. They do not have a direct linkage to any spiritual or religious practice. The fundamental concepts behind Yin and Yang and the Five Elements, however, do have a place in Taoist philosophy.

NOTE FROM JEN: *I fully encourage you to incorporate whatever practices you personally see fit into your practice. I won't discourage you from using them, or force you to choose one or the other. My aim here is simply to eliminate the confusion around the true meaning of Feng Shui, so that you can delineate what is authentic and mainstream, honor the traditions, and incorporate your own personal beliefs at the same time.*

About the Author

Jen Nicomedes is the Founder and Owner of **Feng Shui by Jen®**, providing intimate and personally tailored Feng Shui consulting services for both residences and small businesses.

Jen's unique background and extensive training in both Classical and Contemporary Feng Shui enable her to merge the benefits from both systems to design a fun, practical, and authentic approach to creating a harmonious and meaningful living space for her clients. She is passionate about sharing the Feng Shui experience. She enjoys using her knowledge on the positive effects of this ancient practice to help people cultivate a strong sense of awareness about themselves, their belongings, and their environment.

Throughout the year, Jen partners with local business owners to organize Feng Shui workshops in the Phoenix-Metro Valley and in other U.S. cities. Creating a relaxed space for curious and like-minded beginners and enthusiasts to gather is an important extension of Jen's work as a Feng Shui coach. Moreover, she is also certified to teach a professional Feng Shui course for those seeking to deepen their understanding or to endeavor in a career in Feng Shui.

She is an Associate Member of the International Feng Shui Association and a Board Member for the Arizona Holistic Chamber of Commerce.

Jen trained with world-renowned Feng Shui and BaZi teacher, researcher, and lecturer **Grand Master Raymond Lo** in Hong Kong, while studying abroad in places like Singapore, Dubai, and Tokyo. Grand Master Lo continues to mentor Jen in all areas of Chinese Metaphysics, including Classical Feng Shui, BaZi, and I Ching Divination. In 2013, Jen was hand-picked by Grand Master Lo to be his official representative of the Raymond Lo School of Feng Shui and Destiny in the United States – an honorary title not held by anyone else in the country. Jen's certifications with Grand Master Lo are endorsed by the **International Feng Shui Association** based in Singapore.

Jen is also a certified Essential Feng Shui® Practitioner from the Western School of Feng Shui and Feng Shui-certified with the **Mastery Academy of Chinese Metaphysics** in Kuala Lumpur, Malaysia.

Her background is in corporate accounting. Today, her Feng Shui business, real estate work, and writing offer so much more heart and spirit because she understands what it means to work hard for something you absolutely love. Her passion and view of the world and people around her are reflected in her consultations, her writing, and her work. And she genuinely cares about the success and growth of her clients and those she is blessed to work with.

Made in the USA
San Bernardino, CA
01 October 2017